WHEN THE PROMISE WAS BROKEN

an anthology of short plays
inspired by the songs of Bruce Springsteen

Other titles by Joan Herrington

Playwrights Teach Playwriting (Smith and Kraus)
Playwrights Teach Playwriting 2 (Smith and Kraus)
The Playwrights Muse (Routledge)
I Ain't Sorry for Nothin' I Done: August Wilson's Process of Playwriting (Limelight)
August Wilson in an Hour (Smith and Kraus)

WHEN THE PROMISE WAS BROKEN

an anthology of short plays
inspired by the songs of Bruce Springsteen

edited by: Joan Herrington

Smith and Kraus   2018

A Smith and Kraus Book
177 Lyme Road, Hanover, NH 03755
editorial 603.643.6431 To Order 1.877.668.8680
www.smithandkraus.com

When the Promise Was Broken
Copyright © 2018 by Joan Herrington

Manufactured in the United States of America

ISBN: 9781575259291
Library of Congress Control Number: 2018941900

Typesetting and layout by Elizabeth E. Monteleone
Cover by Emily Herrington
Cover photo by Glynnis Jones/Bigstock.com

For information about custom editions, special sales, education and corporate purchases, please contact Smith and Kraus at editor@smithandkraus.com or 603.643.6431.

For over forty-five years, Bruce Springsteen's music, lyrics and performances have been an ongoing conversation with his audiences worldwide. This project is an opportunity for some of his fans—who are playwrights—to hold up our end of the conversation.

This book would not have been possible without the remarkable work of our editorial assistant, Darcy Sturges and the support of Western Michigan University's College of Fine Arts.

Contents

FOREWORD

From the chorus of nymphs in *Prometheus Bound,* the Theban elders in *Oedipus Rex* and Bottom's love song in *A Midsummer Night's Dream* to Wagner's *Ring*, *Hair,* and *Hamilton*, music has been so deeply embedded in theater that the distinction may be more illusion than reality. That was never truer than in the New York City of the late 1960s and 1970s, where Bruce Springsteen began his ascent. It was a scene suffused with energy: the jazz and soul rituals of the Black Arts Theater, the minimalist phantasmagoria of *Einstein on the Beach.* On the rock 'n' roll side of a very long street, Holy Modal Rounder drummer Sam Shepard's *Cowboy Mouth* pushed the envelope with a vernacular gunfight between Slim and Cavale, played by a young Patti Smith, who would later collaborate with Bruce on one of his most dramatic songs, "Because the Night."

All of which is to say that there's something almost inevitable (and at the same time strikingly original) about this book of plays based on Springsteen's music. Or, more accurately, call these plays *responses.* Springsteen's aesthetic has always been grounded in the African American practice of "call and response." The call and response process is initiated when an artist—musician, writer, painter, dancer—creates something in response to his/her world. It can be political, personal, intellectual, emotional: part of forging a response is deciding what part of the world demands attention. When the artist presents the call to an audience or community, the individual responses become calls of their own, energizing the process that allows a community to make sense of what's going on. That's the foundation of Springsteen's concerts, an interaction with the crowd that transforms it from consumers into participants.

When the Promise Was Broken extends that aesthetic in an important way. Each of the playwrights is responding to Springsteen, but they're simultaneously calling on their readers (and, as we'll get back to, potential theatrical audiences) to respond to *both* the plays and to Springsteen's generative call, which itself calls on us to respond to the world and to each other's responses. It's a matter of inviting "I"s to participate in a communal "we."

That's particularly important since so many of the plays, and Springsteen's songs, focus precisely on isolation, lost hope. Often that revolves around misunderstandings, broken communication. As I read, I found myself thinking of Springsteen's 1997 interview with Will Percy. Reflecting on the evolution of his songwriting, Springsteen said: "In most of the recent songs, I tell violent stories very quietly. You're hearing characters' thoughts—what they're thinking after all the events that have shaped their situation have transpired. So I try to get that internal sound, like that feeling at night when you're in bed and staring at the ceiling, reflective in some fashion. I wanted the songs to have the kind of intimacy that took you inside yourself and then back out into the world."

Springsteen was describing *The Ghost of Tom Joad,* but the words apply equally well too many of the songs on *Darkness on the Edge of Town*, *Nebraska* and *Magic*. I'm sure the playwrights whose work is collected in *When the Promise Was Broken* join in the choruses of "Born to Run" and "Badlands" at Springsteen concerts but their plays gravitate towards Bruce's quieter moments. Like Bruce, they're fascinated by characters reflecting on what's gone wrong with their lives, wondering why they're not quite able to connect with the people they want to love, sometimes catching a glimpse of how those "personal" feelings are shaped by political and economic forces they don't quite understand.

Situations like those Springsteen described occupy the center of more than half of the plays in *When the Promise Was Broken.* In Edward Allan Baker's *The Merry-Go-Round Man,* Arcangelo and Beetle's names point to a struggle between spiritual and physical that would be at home in "Spirit in the Night." The play builds to Beetles desperate claim that "we're good people tryin' to do what we can with what we have, and this past mistake you've brought to this house will not affect what little of the future we have left." In Nikkole Salter's *Birthday Wishes*, inspired by "Secret Garden," a mother and son play out a variation on family tensions that Springsteen wove into the spoken introduction to "The River" that provided the emotional touchstone of his early 1980s concerts.

Differences in age, gender or sexuality don't change the fundamental dynamics. K. Frithjof Peterson's *Pick Up Beds* revolves around a two lovers, Jim and Mark as their relationship winds to an end; even the gestures toward support and solace contribute to the sense of an unbridgeable gap. Responding to Springsteen's Oscar-winning title song for *Philadelphia,* and, subtly, to the AIDS crisis that inspired it, Dipika Guha's *Philadelphia* works heart-breaking variations on the loneliness theme, intensified by the weight of aging and time.

While most of the plays in *When the Promise Was Broken* focus on relationships and psychological themes, a few foreground political and spiritual themes. Responding to "We Take Care of our Own," Peter Ullian's *Valhalla Correctional* empathizes with Lev and Jess as they face the economic and marital problems like those pervading the devastated economies of "The River" or "Youngstown." As Jess asks: "Do you know what it's like? Do you know how emotionally debilitating it is to give fifteen years to a place and then be dumped? You know how that makes a personal feel?" Constructed around a conversation between an African American priest and an Irish American officer devastated by her involvement in a police shooting, Elaine Romero's *Bloody River* calls on us to fundamentally rethink the politics and spiritual implications of what's become an all-too-familiar narrative. Written in response to "Terry's Song," Jennifer Blackmer's *Object Permanence*, offers a searching meditation on the metaphysical implications of human separation. "Nothing is permanent," Terry, an Iraq veteran, muses to his brother Mitch. "The truth is that people DO disappear when they go around a corner, or hide behind a wall. Or go out for morning patrol. Or

3

diffuse an IED. I read somewhere that the human body replaces itself every seven years—every damn cell in my body is new at some point over seven years, so I couldn't have been the same person I was when I enlisted."

Even when a Springsteen song provides characters or the outline of a plot, each of the plays in *When the Promise Was Broken* offers a new perspective on the material. Scott T. Barsotti's *The Stray* retains the central characters of "Highway Patrolman," but his imagination of the tangled relation between Frank, Joe and Maria is absolutely distinctive. Tucker Rafferty's *Glad for the Company*, set in an abandoned prison store room, consists of a searing soliloquy. Its climax juxtaposes the mythic depth of "Adam Raised a Cain" with "Nebraska"'s vision of the "meanness in this world."

One of the most impressive things about these plays is the range of ways they incorporate musical aesthetics into their forms. Echoing the feverish intensity of "I'm on Fire," Greg Moses' *a semi-autobiographical response to feelings of sexual inadequacy prompted by repeatedly listening to Bruce Springsteen's 'I'm on Fire' over and over for like four hours straight* is built around a series of seven vignettes tracking the rising and falling of asymmetrical unfulfilled (and unfulfillable) desires. Dan and Drew Caffrey's *Gospel Hour* with its echoes of "Open All Night," emphasizes the distances between its characters by placing a "live" state trooper in conversation with the voices of two women fading in and out on his cruiser's radio. Sentences decay intro phrases, fragments, noise. It's not clear even, or especially, to the characters who's trying to talk to who. Time slips in memory and what emerges is a shared song welling up from the depths of memory where love and the potential for violence, mostly emotional, but at least potentially physical lurk. If I was staging it, I'd make sure the audience was aware of the trooper's gun. Then again, it's not hard to imagine it as a chillingly effective radio play relying entirely on voice and rhythm.

It's an article of faith amongst Springsteen fans that, while the records are good, they pale in relation to his live performances. Same goes for the relation between script and live theater. As I read, I found myself imagining an evening based on *When the Promise Was Broken.* Putting it together would present the same kinds of challenges and joys as arranging songs on an album, something Springsteen has talked about at length. Taking my cue from the multiple variations of song lists for *Darkness on the Edge of Town* and *The River* included in Bruce's notebooks, I came up with line-ups including pretty much every play. Here's the one I'd commit to, at least today: Steve Feffer's *Growin' Up: Or, I was a Teenage Bruce Springsteen!*; Greg Moses' *semi-autobiographical response* and Steven Dietz's *Drive All Night.*

The central concern of that evening would be the ways voice, tonalities and variations on the call and response structure add depth and dimension to words and lyrics. Several of my favorite Springsteen songs—"Something in the Night," "The Price You Pay," the underappreciated blue-eyed soul of *Human Touch*—draw their power from Springsteen's use of the African American practice of the *moan* (a.k.a. melisma or vocalization). It's a way of tapping into complexities of experience, drawing on a depth of emotion that resists reduction to words. You hear the communal version in the "oh-oh-oh's" that rise up from the crowd when the E-Street Band plays "Badlands" or "Thunder Road" live.

Each of the plays in my line up offers a different angle on call and response. Funny and exuberant, Feffer's *Growin' Up* excavates one genealogy of Bruce's voice in a set of rollicking interchanges involving the "Cosmic Kid" and two archetypal incarnations of Elvis Presley: the young Elvis whose music called Springsteen on his path and the late-period Elvis who has served as a cautionary example as Springsteen has both shaped and resisted his own myth. Beginning with its note-perfect title, Greg Moses' *a semi-autobiographical response to feelings of sexual inadequacy prompted by repeatedly listening to Bruce Springsteen's "I'm on Fire" over and over for like four hours straight* brilliantly links the internal and external aspects of call and response. Thinking of the five sections as "a series of comic strip panels," the protagonist fumbles his way from thought to voice, making an absolute hash of his calls to a lover as she works through her own psychic and erotic complexities.

I know this will change over time, but the play that drew the strongest response from me after the first few readings was Steve Dietz's *Drive All Night*. The backbone of the play is provided by a sequence of sections where Vi and the people crowding her life and memory repeat simple, almost primal, phrases: a nameless man's "I got— to see you" answered by Vi's" "no," "please don't," and "don't say that." Jackie and Vi trading "Where are you", each one of which would sound different in performance. Jackie's aching response to Vi's "Then he left. He just left": "He left. He left. He left. He left. He left," building back to Vi's "The more you say it, the less true it gets." Which both is and isn't true.

Those plays would make for a dynamic night of theater. But it's just one of countless equally compelling possibilities. Something like 80% of my imaginary playbills included either *Bloody River* or *Gospel Hour*, frequently both. A single night of theater based on *When the Promise Was Broken* wouldn't get the job done. Let's make it a festival. You could put together nights focusing on religion and spirituality, on romance and sexuality, on politics and economics. As you read, think and feel your way through the infinite possibilities of the calls echoing through *When the Promise Was Broken,* imagine your own, visualize the characters and the settings, hear their voices. Respond.

—Craig Werner

THE PLAYWRIGHTS

EDWARD ALLAN BAKER is a published and frequently produced NYC playwright, his one act plays are produced all over U.S., Canada, Europe, and Australia, the most notable is *Dolores*, translated into 5 languages. Other one-acts of note include, *North of Providence, Rosemary with Ginger, Mafia on Prozac, Face Divided,*and *'Up, Down, Strange, Charmed, Beauty and Truth.'* His produced full-length plays include, *Prairie Avenue, The Framer, American Storage, Free Gift Inside, Sonny Under the Assumption,* and *East of Heart Mountain* (among others). Mr.Baker adapted his Plays, *Dolores, Rosemary with Ginger,* and *Face Divided* for the screen, and a Spanish version of *Dolores* is slated for 2018 release. He teaches at The Actors Studio Drama School MFA Program at Pace University, and a recipient of "The 25th Anniversary Award for Theatrical Excellence," from the iconic Ensemble Studio Theatre of NYC. He is a member of The Dramatists Guild.

SCOTT T. BARSOTTI is a writer from Pittsburgh. He is the author of the novel *Single Version*; his full-length plays include *Brewed, The Revenants, Jet Black Chevrolet, Kill Me, Facing Angela*, and *Entry (or, you think you know me).* He spent many years in Chicago producing with horror company WildClaw Theatre.

JENNIFER BLACKMER is the 2015 PEN/Laura Pels International Foundation for Theatre Award winner for Emerging American Playwright. Her plays have been seen across the country and include *Human Terrain*, *Unraveled*, Margaret Atwood's *Alias Grace*, *Delicate Particle Logic,* and *Borrowed Babies.* Jennifer's screenplay for *Human Terrain* won the prestigious Alfred P. Sloan Foundation award through the Tribeca Film Institute, and was also a finalist for the Sundance Film Institute Sloan Prize. Jennifer's writing has been short-listed for the Princess Grace Award and the Shakespeare's Sister Fellowship, and has been developed by Seven Devils, Illinois Shakespeare Festival, Nashville Repertory Theatre, The Playwrights' Center, The Lark and Activate Midwest. Jennifer is a Professor of Theatre and Associate Provost at Ball State University.

9

DAN CAFFREY is an M.F.A. in Playwriting Candidate at UT Austin's Department of Theatre and Dance. Before UT, he spent almost 11 years in Chicago, where he was an Associate Artist with the side project, an Ensemble Member of The Ruckus (RIP), and served as Founding Artistic Director for the Tympanic Theatre Company (RIP), who produced an entire short-play festival inspired by Bruce Springsteen's *Nebraska*. His play *Matawan* (produced by The Ruckus) was a Finalist for the Eugene O'Neill National Playwrights Conference in 2013 and his play *The Tusk Hunters* was a Semi-Finalist in 2015. In addition to being a playwright, he has written and edited for several publications as a pop-culture critic. His articles have appeared in The A.V. Club, CBR, Pitchfork, Vox, and Consequence of Sound, where he's a Senior Writer and co-hosts *The Losers' Club: A Stephen King Podcast*. Born in New Jersey, he wrote "Gospel Hour" with his dad, Drew, who introduced him to The Boss at a very young age.

DREW CAFFREY was born and raised in New Jersey. Today, he resides in Verona, NJ, with his wife, Janine. He was a New Jersey State Trooper for four years, including 1982, when Bruce Springsteen released *Nebraska*.

STEVEN DIETZ's recent world premieres include *Bloomsday* (2016 Steinberg New Play Award Citation); *This Random World* (40th Humana Festival of New American Plays); and *On Clover Road* (NNPN "rolling world premiere"). Other recent work includes *Rancho Mirage* (Edgerton New Play Award), *The Shimmering,* and *American la Ronde.* A two-time winner of the Kennedy Center Fund for New American Plays Award *(Fiction, Still Life with Iris),* Dietz is also a two-time finalist for the American Theater Critic's Steinberg New Play Award *(Last of the Boys*, *Becky's New Car).* He received the PEN USA West Award in Drama for *Lonely Planet*, and the 2007 Edgar Award for Drama for *Sherlock Holmes: The Final Adventure.* Other widely produced plays and adaptations include *Yankee Tavern, Jackie & Me, Shooting Star, Dracula, Inventing van Gogh, God's Country, Private Eyes*, and *The Nina Variations.*

STEVE FEFFER's plays have been produced or developed by theatres that include the Eugene O'Neill National Playwrights Conference, Ensemble Studio Theatre, Untitled Theatre #61's International Festival of Jewish Theatre, Stages Repertory Theatre (Houston), Victory Gardens Theatre (Chicago), Ruckus Theatre (Chicago), and Whole Art and Fancy Pants Theatres (Kalamazoo), among numerous others. Steve's play "The Origins of the Drink They Named After Me" is published in *Best American Short Plays 2012-13* (Applause Books). His play "And Yet…" is published in *Best American Short Plays 2010-11* (Applause Books); and "Little Airplanes of the Heart" is published in *Best American Short Plays 1997-98* (Applause Books) and *Plays from Ensemble Studio Theatre 2000* (Faber and Faber). Dramatists Play Service publishes his play *The Wizards of Quiz*; Heinemann Books, Smith and Kraus, and New Issues Press have published additional theatre pieces. Steve has won a number of national playwriting awards including twice being awarded the New Jewish Theatre Project Award from the Foundation for Jewish Culture, the Jamie Hammerstein Award from Ensemble Studio Theatre, and the Southwest Play Award for a Play for Young Audiences. He has served on the National Executive Committee for the Kennedy Center's National Playwriting Program of the American College Theatre Festival and directs the undergraduate and graduate play-writing programs at Western Michigan University, Kalamazoo, MI. "This play is dedicated to the memory of my mom and dad, Myrna and Gordon Feffer. To paraphrase Bruce: Tonight you're both going to have to settle for rock 'n' roll."

DIPIKA GUHA was born in India and raised in Russia and the United Kingdom. Her plays include *Yoga Play* (South Coast Repertory, The Kilroys' List '17) and *The Art of Gaman* (Ground Floor, Berkeley Repertory Theatre, The Kilroys' List '16) and *Mechanics of Love* (Crowded Fire Theatre). She was the inaugural recipient of the Shakespeare's Sister Award through the Lark Play Development Center, A Room of Her Own and Hedgebrook and is a Hodder Fellow at Princeton University. Guha is writing plays for Manhattan Theatre Club, South Coast

Repertory, Barrington Stage and Oregon Shakespeare Festival, amongst others. Dipika received her MFA from the Yale School of Drama. For television, she has written for the series adaptation of Neil Gaiman's novel *American Gods* on Starz and *Paradise Lost* for AMC.

GREGORY S. MOSS is a writer, educator and performer from Newburyport MA. He holds an MFA in Dramatic Writing from Brown University's Literary Arts Program. He is an Assistant Professor of Theatre and helms the MFA in Dramatic Writing at the University of New Mexico. Gregory is a 2012 MacDowell Fellow, an Affiliated Artist with Clubbed Thumb, a member of SPACE at Ryder Farm's inaugural Working Farm writers group, and the recipient of a 2010-2011 Jerome Fellowship and a 2011-2012 McKnight Fellowship. Recent: *punkplay* at The Southwark Playhouse, London; world premiere of *Indian Summer* at Playwrights' Horizons (Critics' Pick, *Time Out New York*); "*I Promised Myself to Live Faster*": *A Queer Space Opera in the Decadent Style*, Actor's Theatre of Louisville; *Reunion* at South Coast Rep (Best New Play of 2014, *OC Weekly* and *Stage Source LA*); *House of Gold* at La Comédie Française, Paris (winner, Prix du Public), Square Product Theatre, CO, and EST-LA (*LA Times* and *LA Weekly* Critics' Pick).

K. FRITHJOF PETERSON's work has been performed throughout the United States as well as translated and performed in Moscow, Russia. Full length plays include *Where the Whang-doodle Sings* (Generous Company), *Bookmarks* (Seven Devil Playwrights Conference) and *Bosons*. His plays have also been finalists for The O'Neill National Playwrights Conference, The Kennedy Center's National Ten-Minute Play Award, the Heideman Award, and the Samuel French OOB Festival and developed with The Kennedy Center, WordBRIDGE, Seven Devils, Fusion Theatre Company (Albuquerque), The Inkwell (D.C.), Strange Sun Theater (NYC), The Gift Theatre (Chicago), Williams Street Rep (IL) and Fox Valley Rep (IL).

TUCKER RAFFERTY has been a professional theatre artist for over thirty years, serving as an actor with over one hundred stage credits, as a director with over fifty credits, and as a playwright with his plays being seen all over the country including his hometown of Kalamazoo, Chicago and New York. Recently Tucker's play *Why Dogs Howl* was honored at the Michigan Playwrights Festival. For twenty years Tucker has been employed by KRESA's Education For The Arts, teaching different forms of playwriting. Tucker was also the Producing Artistic Director of Kalamazoo's Whole Art Theatre. He has a B.A. from Western Michigan University and lives in Kalamazoo with his daughter Hannah.

ELAINE ROMERO is an award-winning U.S. playwright. Her plays have been presented across the U.S. and abroad, and widely published and anthologized. *Graveyard of Empires* and *A Work of Art* recently premiered. *Title IX* was included in the 2017 Eugene O›Neill National Playwrights Conference. *Modern Slave* was presented at the 2017 Seven Devils Playwrights Conference where Romero was the Featured Playwright. *Modern Slave* was given a reading in Seattle in a collaboration between eSe Teatro and A Contemporary Theatre. It received previous readings at Victory Gardens Theater and The Road Theatre. Romero's work has been published by Samuel French, Playscripts, Simon and Schuster, among others. Elaine is a Resident Playwright at Chicago Dramatists and an Assistant Professor at the University of Arizona in the School of Theatre, Film, and Television. She splits her time between Tucson and Chicago. She is a long-time Playwright-in-Residence at Arizona Theatre Company.

NIKKOLE SALTER began her professional career with her co-authorship and co-performance (with Danai Gurira) of the Pulitzer Prize nominated play, *In the Continuum* (ITC) for which she received an Obie, NY Outer Critics', and the Global Tolerance Award from the Friends of the United Nations. Since then, Ms. Salter's plays have been produced on three continents, published in 12 international publications, and broadcast on the WNET program "Theatre Close-Up." As an actress she has graced the big and small screen and performed theatrically with renowned directors, including TONY nominated Liesl Tommy and winner Kenny Leon. www.nikkolesalter.com

PETER ULLIAN's work for the stage has been produced off-Broadway, regionally, and internationally. Critics have praised his work as "singularly satisfying, winning, heart rending, punchy, button-pushing, irresistible" (*The New York Times*), "taut, absorbing, a joyful accomplishment" (*Variety*), and "a cross between David Mamet and the Marx Brothers" (*The Cleveland Plain Dealer*). He has worked with some of the world's top theatre directors, including Harold Prince, David Esbjornson, and Lynne Taylor-Corbett. His short stories have appeared in magazines and anthologies, and he has written screenplays for major motion picture and independent studios. His plays *Big Bossman* and *The Triumphant Return of Blackbird Flynt* are both published by Broadway Play Publishing. His short play, *Waiting for Marcel*, is jointly published by the International Writing Program/University of Cape Town/Artscape Theatre Centre/African Arts Institute as part of *Book Wings South Africa*. His acclaimed musical, *Flight of the Lawnchair Man*, is published by Theatrical Rights Worldwide. He has received awards from the Kennedy Center Fund for New American Plays and the Gilman & Gonzalez-Falla Musical Theater Foundation, as well as production grants from the National Endowment for the Arts and the New York Foundation for the Arts. He has received commissions for new work from the Iowa Cultural Council, En Garde Arts, the Prince Music Theatre, the Denver Theatre Center, The Directors Company, and Snap Two Productions. He has taught dramatic writing at Hollins University and University of Wisconsin-Green Bay, and creative writing at SUNY Old Westbury. He is a graduate of Oberlin College and the University of Iowa Playwrights Workshop. He has been a fan of Bruce Springsteen since he first heard "Born to Run" while riding in the back of his parents' station wagon.

CRAIG WERNER long-time member of the Nominating Committee of the Rock and Roll Hall of Fame and is the author of *A Change Is Gonna Come: Music, Race and the Soul of America*; *Up Around the Bend: An Oral History of Creedence Clearwater Revival*, and *We Gotta Get Out of This Place: The Soundtrack of Vietnam* (co-authored with Doug Bradley) which was *Rolling Stone*'s Best Music Book of 2015.

Drive All Night

By Steven Dietz

Inspired by "Drive All Night" by Bruce Springsteen

CHARACTERS

VI: A woman, mid-life.

JACKIE: A woman, mid-life.

A MAN: Same age.

SETTING

A bar—evoked only, not fully rendered.

A car—same.

A Bar.

*A woman, VI, sits at the end of a long dimly-lit bar.
She holds a drink.*

*At the other end of the bar, not looking at VI, is another
WOMAN.*

She also holds a drink. We cannot yet see her face.

There is no bartender.

VI speaks to the audience.

VI: *(to the audience)*I got you. I got. I got. I got you. So soft.
Like that. I got you, Vi. My Violet.

I got.

Got.

Got you.

She drinks.

I'm the idiot. To fall for that shit. That "I got you. I got you,
my pretty Violet." I fell for that shit.

I fell for the look in his pretty brown eyes.

And then it got worse.

Then I missed him.

Missed him saying those things with his pretty brown eyes.

And then it got worse.

I called him.

And he said ...

A Car. Night.

The MAN is driving. He is alone.

MAN: Wait for me. Please wait for me, Vi.

VI: Why on earth would I do that?

MAN: Because I'm on my way.

VI: Where are you?

MAN: I'm far. I'm too far.

VI: Where?

MAN: I doesn't matter. I'm driving. I'm gonna drive all night. As long as it takes.

VI: Yes - okay - but —

MAN: I got —

VI: No.

MAN: I got —

VI: Please don't.

MAN: I got to see you.

VI: Don't say that —

MAN: I got to hold you in my arms.

> *Pause.*

VI: *(to audience)* And then it got worse.

MAN: Did you hear me?

VI: I said: Okay.

MAN: See you soon.

> *The MAN continues to drive, as —*
>
> *The other woman at the bar turns to the audience. This is JACKIE.*

JACKIE: *(to the audience)* "It doesn't matter, baby. Wait for me. Wait for me as a long as it takes. Cause I'm driving, baby. I'm always driving home to you."

And I say don't call me baby. I'm not your baby. I'm not anyone's baby. And he stops. He stops calling me that. He stops saying anything at all.

And I wait.

I look in his eyes - those china blue eyes - those goddamn china blue eyes - and I say ...

It's not gonna work. Not this time. Drive all you want. But don't come here. And don't call me baby.

And he stares at me.

And I wish I'd said more.

I wish I'd said something.

Even one thing.

Because I didn't. I hadn't. I hadn't said a word of it.

In my head I had told him off - set him straight - laid down the law. In my head I had told him in no uncertain terms: "nope - no way - not gonna work - I'm not your baby - and don't you dare come see me again."

But on the phone...I said nothing.

And he said nothing.

But neither of us hung up.

All I could hear was the sound of his car.

He drove for hours.

I sat on the roof of my building, the phone cradled to my ear ...

Listening to the roar of the road.

MAN: *(as he drives)* Vi. My Violet. Are you there?

VI: I'm always here. You know that.

MAN: Good.

VI: And I'm never here. You know that.

MAN: Sure you are.

VI: I'm always with you.

MAN: Good.

VI: And I'm never with you. Where are you? When will you be here?

MAN: Soon.

Pause.

VI: That's a terrible word. Don't say that word again.

MAN: Why?

VI: It's a cruel word that sounds kind.

Moon, spoon, June...those are all sweet and kind words.
But not "soon." Soon is a tease and a taunt. Soon is out to hurt you.

JACKIE: You said soon.

MAN: Did I?

JACKIE: You always say soon.

MAN: And I mean it. I always mean it.

JACKIE: Who is she? Who's the other one?

MAN: No one.

JACKIE: Bullshit.

MAN: Just you.

JACKIE: Did you play "Heart and Soul" with her?

MAN: Just you.

JACKIE: Did she play the right hand and did you play the left?

MAN: Just you.

JACKIE: Did you kill that song - like we did? Did you crack that room in two?

MAN: Just you.

VI: Bullshit.

MAN: Just you.

VI: The more you say it —

MAN: Just you.

VI: — the less true it gets.

JACKIE: Or was it just me?

MAN: Just you.

VI: Because you've got —

JACKIE: And one car.

MAN: Yes.

VI: Got —

JACKIE: One road.

MAN: Yes.

VI: Got —

JACKIE: One night.

MAN: Yes.

VI: — you've got to tell me —

JACKIE: What do you see?

MAN: Where?

VI: — right now —

JACKIE: Right now - out the window of your car —

VI: — where are you?

JACKIE: — what is there? What are you seeing right now?

VI: You never say where you are —

JACKIE: I've got to know.

VI: — you always just say you're "close."

MAN: I'm close.

VI: *(with a laugh)* Fuck you.

JACKIE: What are you seeing?

MAN: I'm seeing you, baby.

JACKIE: *(with a laugh)* Fuck you.

VI: You can't always be "close."

MAN: Sure I can.

VI: If you keep being "close" - one day you have to be here.

JACKIE: Tell me —

VI: Tell me —

MAN: Through the wind.

VI: — c'mon - you can give me this —

MAN: Through the snow.

JACKIE: — you can tell me this —

MAN: Through the rain.

JACKIE: Where are you?

VI: Where are you?

JACKIE: Where are you?

VI: Where are you?

JACKIE: Where are you?

VI: Where are you?

JACKIE: Where are you?

VI: Where are you?

JACKIE: Where are you?

VI: Where are you? Where are you? Where are you?

> *Pause.*

VI: (cont'd)Where are you?

> *Pause.*

JACKIE: Where are you?

> *The MAN has vanished.*

> *Silence.*

VI: And he's gone.

And I'm alone.

JACKIE: And I don't know where he is.

VI: I just know ...

JACKIE: All I want to know ...

VI: I just know ...

JACKIE: ... is that he's on his way.

VI: ... he's on his way to me.

JACKIE: That is delicious.

VI: That's all I need.

> *Pause.*

JACKIE: But then it gets better —

VI: And better yet —

JACKIE: — because I know about her.

VI: — he has chosen me.

JACKIE: I know she's waiting for him too.

VI: But why —

JACKIE: But what she doesn't know —

VI: — why does knowing that make it feel even better?

JACKIE: — is that he's driving all through the night for me.

> *They sip their drinks.*
>
> *Pause. Then ...*
>
> *LOUD KNOCKING is heard.*
>
> *They each slowly set their drinks on the bar.*

VI: And then it gets worse.

JACKIE: He arrives.

> *The KNOCKING STOPS. And now ...*
>
> *VI and JACKIE turn and speak to each other for the first time in the play.*
>
> *The distance remains between them.*

VI: You thought you made him up.

JACKIE: I did make him up. And so did you.

VI: Yes —

JACKIE: You thought that too, right?

VI: — of course I did. I don't want him knocking on my door!

JACKIE: I just want him driving!

VI: Yes!

JACKIE: I just want him to never really arrive.

But there he was. I could hear him on the other side of the door.

VI: I looked through the peephole.

JACKIE: I did too.

VI: And there he stood. He had this bag. And inside this bag there were boxes.

JACKIE: They were shoes.

VI: What the hell?

JACKIE: They were shoes.

VI: I know. But what the hell?

JACKIE: Why is he bringing me shoes ...?

VI: He left them.

JACKIE: I don't want him bringing me shoes!

VI: He left them at the door.

JACKIE: Left the goddamn shoes.

VI: And then he left. He just left.

JACKIE: He left. He left. He left. He left. He left.

VI: The more you say it —

JACKIE: He left.

VI: — the less true it gets.

A long silence. They sip their drinks.

VI: (cont'd) Mom used to say: Be sure to fall in love with what you're never going to have. That way you can't be disappointed.

Pause.

JACKIE: Mom used to say: People are not in love with love. They are in love with longing.

Love fades. Love grows thin.

But longing...longing only deepens.

Pause.

VI: I like your shoes.

JACKIE: Thank you.

Pause.

VI: You sure you didn't let him in? Didn't open the door?

JACKIE: Why would I do that? I've got him right where I want him.

In my head. In that car. Driving all night.

The MAN is seen once again. It is night. He is driving.

VI: He had a good left hand.

JACKIE: On "Heart and Soul"?

Yes, he did.

Yes, he did.

VI: We cracked that room in two.

The image of the TWO WOMEN fades, as —

The MAN continues to drive.

End of Play.

Bloody River

By Elaine Romero

Inspired by "American Skin" by Bruce Springsteen

CHARACTERS

THERESA/OFFICER/SHOOTER: 34. Irish-American woman.

MASON: 40's. A plain-clothes priest. African-American.

TIME: Present

PLACE: Cathedral

LOCATION: Urban America

OFFICER enters the cathedral, kneels and prays at the foot of the altar, visibly upset, harried, stuck somewhere in that place between immediate aftermath and lifelong regret.

A baptismal font sits on the altar. Officer crosses to it, reaches into her holster and lifts up the gun, dunking it in the baptismal font, pouring holy water over it, wringing and washing her bloody hands.

She returns to the pew, takes out a rosary to pray. It's a prayer long forgotten. She struggles to begin.

OFFICER: "Hail Mary, full of grace, the Lord is with *me*.

She seems relieved to have knocked out the first sentence though she got it wrong.

OFFICER: Blessed art thou amongst women—"

She laughs—self-irony—a lady cop with bloody hands and a bloody gun. She gets lost mid-prayer, stops herself, wrestling to create a quiet moment. She stands, reaches into her empty holster, and we see why she has come. It's as if she has a gun, shoots and shoots and shoots. She sits down again. Prayer can't save her now. She crosses back to the baptismal font, and commits the unsacred act of lifting the gun to her head.

She can't do it.

MASON, the plainclothes priest, enters.

MASON: Don't. It would disturb God.

Officer looks truly startled, looks down at the gun.

The first of forty-one gunshots begins. They linger in the distance and will go off and reverberate throughout the play.

Wars rage. People starve.

OFFICER: Strokes strike good people in the head at the prime of their lives and they struggle to speak and move.

31

Officer stares at Mason but he has nothing to say.

Officer gets the gun up high again.

OFFICER: Clearly, you are mistaken, Sir. God, your God, is not easily disturbed.

MASON: You describe the mystery of God.

OFFICER: Indifferent, maybe. An asshole, probably.

MASON: God forgives. Plain as that.

OFFICER: Your God is kinder than mine.

MASON: To live with a punishing God in one's mind is to live a life of hell.

Officer chortles.

OFFICER: Some people say, God, your God, created this whole mess and threw us on the planet to duke it out.

We're all just gladiators, fighting to the death. For His eternal amusement.

He makes us eat his only kid and drink his bloody blood and He is not disturbed.

MASON: It's a baptismal font. Used to clean the stain of original sin. And in the same way, the sacrifice of Jesus Christ on the cross—

Look, whatever you've done—God, Christ—

This triggers Officer and she puts the gun closer to her head. More shots in the distance, but it's as if she has already heard them.

OFFICER: You sound like one of them.

MASON: I came here to pray.

OFFICER: Don't mind me. I'm sure God can silence the sound of gunfire in your pious ears.

Awkward silence as they pray.

More shots in the night.

OFFICER: Are you praying yet?

MASON: I heard once that when a prayer begins, it never ends. It just rolls on in the background.

OFFICER: Like a never-ending scroll?

The Father doth protest too much.

MASON: God is a God of forgiveness.

OFFICER: Is that why you're here?

MASON: God teaches us to forgive ourselves when we can't. That's the mystery. If you are able to find some kind of intrinsic belief, God can teach us when we can no longer move—when we fail. When we fall down. God lifts us up and says, "I forgive you, my son. My daughter."

OFFICER: To have one particle of your belief—

MASON: Belief is not so hard. It's the maintenance. The watering and the—

OFFICER: Fertilizer. Say it. Fertilizer. The shit. Belief takes a lot of bullshit. Shit we don't have time for. Shit we don't want to get on our hands. But it takes a lot of schlepping of shit to make God's garden grown. He doesn't forgive us without making us suf-fer.

Mason looks baffled. A smile struggles to remain hidden. A long beat.

OFFICER: There'd been a rape. Stranger rape. A young woman. She said it was a black man who did it. Didn't get a good look. So, when we saw him, the suspect—-we told him to raise his hands. Simple instructions. And he didn't. Do that. He did not raise his hands so they would be in plain sight.

MASON: And seeing is believing in your profession.

OFFICER: Officers get shot by suspects every day. He starts reaching around. Finger bulging from his pocket. It could have been a gun. It could have been a knife. I shot first. And then everybody else just kept shooting and shooting. He was on the ground and we were shooting and shooting because he had train-wrecked a soul, and we'd seen the effects of that, being on the force.

Stranger rape. Young girl. Unfair. Can't defend herself. She'll live with him forever in her head.

A life sentence. Rape.

And me. Justice ringing through every bullet. And when the smoke clears, we look at him.

He doesn't look like a rapist at all. Just a young kid, really.

Forty-one shots.

And that is why I take issue with your God. Your God! He is a person, a being—

MASON: Who allowed you to do that? The God who did not rob you of your free will?

She lifts the gun again, but not at herself. Mason remains unafraid.

OFFICER: You should leave now. Only God should have to look on what He has created.

MASON: I offer myself for free.

OFFICER: If you want to kill yourself, you're going to have to muster your own courage.

She threatens him with the gun.

OFFICER: Leave!

MASON: I'm unafraid.

OFFICER: Then, why are you here making your case? Isn't that why we walk into places like this? To make our cases? For heaven and not hell? For mercy? Because when we get on the wrong side of His good mercy, the fucked-up shit starts. And when the shit gets real, there's no way to stop it.

It's like an avalanche of ice coming at you. And instead of moving out of the way, you just let it come on at you even though on some level you know, on some level, you will drown, in ice. You will suffocate. You will live to know that you have truly fucked up. You will be buried alive. But we do it anyway. We stare at our shit, our bullshit, and refuse to get out of the fucking way.

MASON: A woman came to the church daily. Mass. It wasn't a popular thing to do anymore. Lives have gotten busy. People don't come anymore. But she was always here. Father, this. Father, that. I never knew what she did after that. Always dressed up. Always consumed the host right off my hand.

And I didn't notice. I didn't notice. I didn't notice until I noticed. And once I noticed I couldn't stop noticing.

I kneeled next to her to pray one day and I knew. In good conscience, I could not continue to . . .

He wrings a Roman collar in his hand, crosses to the baptismal font and leaves it in there.

OFFICER: You are one of them.

MASON: I'm going to go on retreat — fast and pray, and see.

OFFICER: You already know.

MASON: They've got horses and cactus, picture rocks — cave paintings. Maybe if I stare at the cave picture long enough, the truth will come to me. Maybe there is some truth in the simple lives of caveman.

OFFICER: I don't think the cave dwellers were Catholic.

MASON: And if I fast and pray—

OFFICER: I'm sure the cave dwellers were as complicated as fuck.

MASON: I hold them in high regard.

OFFICER: Does she still come here?

Mason doesn't say.

OFFICER: I think you should follow your heart.

MASON: I should leave this place now.

OFFICER: What I wouldn't give to swap my sins with yours.

You are a gentle soul and gentle souls should not be left to pick up the pieces from what I'm about to do.

MASON: I'm not one to discourage a soul from following her heart—

OFFICER: Except yours.

MASON: —but my replacement, a gentle soul, will find you. It will be him. Newly ordained. They brought him in last week. He is young and eager and full of the fire of God.

OFFICER: The kid's mother was watching from their window. I thought you should know.

I've heard that when God hears your confessions He writes them down on a scroll that leads all the way to infinity. He records your sins, your crimes, for all to see. That's what my great-grandma always said.

And me? I've got too may entries in the scroll of God.

MASON: God, as I understand Him, would never keep score.

OFFICER: Not all God's commandments are created equal.

Lust in your heart. Christ. Make the sign of the cross. Say two Hail Mary's, a couple of Our Father's and you're done.

MASON: I made a vow. And some would say I am held to a higher standard.

OFFICER: His mother watched us murder her son from the window.

MASON: Which only means he was not alone in death. The woman who bore him witnessed his arrival and his departure. God had the mercy to ensure he did not die alone. His mother watched. She watched. She watched. She held him in her eyes and did not let go. He died engulfed in her love.

Officer loosens the gun. This explanation has the possibility of flying.

OFFICER: Yet I've given her irresolvable grief.

Mason takes his time. He knows human suffering.

MASON: The young man will never know the pain of losing his mother. He will not suffer that.

Officer thinks for a second. It appears this might work.

OFFICER: Is that what they teach you in seminary school? How to pull a fast one with logic?

MASON: I am a Jesuit after all.

OFFICER: I think too much for my own good.

MASON: Jesuits don't end it with a gun. They think and ponder and roll over the truth in the palm of their hands, believing, perhaps, if they see it shimmer just right, if they see it from the correct and right perspective, the truth will be revealed.

You did not come here to kill yourself. You're here to understand how you will live with what you've done.

The sound of the forty- first gunshot.

OFFICER: When will those ever end?

MASON: That scroll in your head is not God's, but yours. Your great-grandmother was merely trying to control you, to teach you how to behave, but I'm afraid she left you with an unhelpful metaphor.

Silence for a moment.

OFFICER: *(A statement)* You're leaving God.

MASON: You came back to the church.

Officer hands Mason his now-bloody collar.

OFFICER: You wouldn't want to scare the new guy.

Mason takes it, starts to leave. Officer speaks.

OFFICER: "Bless me, Father, for I have sinned."

Mason stops.

OFFICER: "Bless me, Father, for I have sinned. Bless me, Father, for I have sinned."

Mason turns.

Officer returns to her pew, kneels down, makes the sign of the cross. Mason now stands on the other side of the pew. Maybe he can't give this up quite yet.

OFFICER: "It has been twenty-six years since my last confession."

Officer bows her head. Mason puts his hand on her shoulder, blessing her.

Lights.

End of play.

A SEMI-AUTOBIOGRAPHICAL RESPONSE TO FEELINGS OF SEXUAL INADEQUACY PROMPTED BY REPEATEDLY LISTENING TO BRUCE SPRINGSTEEN'S "I'M ON FIRE" OVER AND OVER FOR FOUR HOURS STRAIGHT

By Gregory S. Moss

Inspired by "I'm on Fire" by Bruce Springsteen

CHARACTERS

NATHAN: late 20 / early 30s.

MARIE: late 20s / early 30s.

MAX: early 30s.

COLIN: earlier late 20s.

SETTING

Somewhere in America.

NATHAN: So first of all this should be told like in a like - like think of all of this as if it was a series of comic strip panels - like one of those Adrian Tomine strips from the New Yorker or - or like a Noah Baumbach movie - just like overlay that style in your imagination over everything that comes next. Ok?

hard cut to Nathan and Marie - in bed post coital pause - they linger in the moment

NATHAN: ...that was - "good" - right?

MARIE: *(pleased)* mm hm

(*pats his back*)

good job

NATHAN: what

MARIE: this is the first time we had sex where you didn't - apologize, or -

NATHAN: - I don't *apologize* -

MARIE: - you didn't say "I'll do better next time" or "I'm sorry" or something

NATHAN: well it was *good* this time

MARIE: It was good from the beginning!

MARIE: yeah but now

we've been doing it for a while, it's been

six weeks

NATHAN: six weeks?

MARIE: six weeks since we first had sex

NATHAN: that was six weeks?

MARIE: it was at my house and you were like

we were making out on the bed and

NATHAN: in your old apartment

MARIE: - right, and you got up and got a condom and I was like, welp, guess we're doing it

NATHAN: you didn't want to?

MARIE: I did I just thought we were waiting

NATHAN: we were waiting

we waited

and then

MARIE: we weren't waiting anymore

pause

NATHAN: yeah well that's what I'm saying

it was fine, I was doing fine

but six weeks is my "sweet spot"

it's where I start to get like

I don't know

I learn what you like

I guess

pause

MARIE: I glad I'm not complaining I like it

NATHAN: maybe you're used to like //

MARIE: here we go //

NATHAN: you're used to like more "adventurous" experiences in bed

MARIE: I'm not

(beat)

I mean

(beat)

I mean I've done some stuff but that's

I'm not looking for that from you

pause

NATHAN: why not

MARIE: what

NATHAN: why not from me

MARIE: because

>   sex is specific to the people right?

>   it's not about replicating some previous //

NATHAN: But I mean I get the sense that

>   maybe I'm more

>   "traditional" than

MARIE: let's not do this

NATHAN: why not

MARIE: it's ruining a good thing it's only gonna make you -

>   you're gonna get weird

NATHAN: I'm not getting weird

>   just

>   like

>   tell me one thing

>   and

>   I'll drop it

MARIE: You'll drop it?

NATHAN: swear to god I promise I'll drop it

>   *pause*

MARIE: this is a bad idea

NATHAN: tell me

>   *pause*

MARIE: ok

>   so

>   this guy I was dating

>   it was before you but this was like

it was months ago like almost two years ago so don't get weird about it

NATHAN: I'm not weird

MARIE: plus I think he moved away

I haven't seen him anywhere in a while so

but

(beat)

he was this punk - gutter punk kid - and we were at some shows together and he really liked me and he was really good at showing it, he was expressive, and it's not like I was crazy about him - he did a lot of coke and was definitely bi-polar or something - but he really liked me and I was at a low point so I said yeah, ok, let's do this.

NATHAN: "do this"?

MARIE: what

NATHAN: date or like - fuck

MARIE: are you getting weird

NATHAN: no! I just like clarity I need you to clarify

MARIE: both

I guess

(pause)

so I was drunk and he was drunk at we were at the Launchpad after some shitty metal show, and I was like yeah, let's

(beat)

so we walk back to my house - I was at the place downtown then -

NATHAN: - and -

MARIE: and we do it and he stays the night and so we start seeing each other. And he was boring, like pretty dumb - I mean his bod was smokin', no doubt about that -

NATHAN: - cool -

MARIE: - that kind of skinny trashy gutter punk bod that always looks pale and like it's bruised up and he had *abs* you// know

NATHAN: cool cool // cool

MARIE: abs that stuck out, and –

just like, withhold judgement -

across his abs he had a tattoo in that. like, gothic script, that like, Motorhead font?, it said...

I can't tell you

NATHAN: come on!

MARIE: I can't believe I dated this guy

NATHAN: come on though tell me

MARIE: ok

so

in that black calligraphy

big letters

he'd tattooed the word "SCUM" across his stomach

pause

NATHAN: "scum"?

MARIE: the word "scum" uh huh

pause

NATHAN: "scum"

pause

NATHAN: was he

did he have like "low self-esteem"? or

MARIE: I think he had like a bad childhood

bad things with his dad and, and the coke and the probably mental illness, so...

(pause)

I'm not proud of it

NATHAN: you don't have to be ashamed of it

MARIE: I didn't say I was ashamed I said I wasn't proud of it.

pause

MARIE: the only thing interesting about him was the sex

pause

MARIE: he

he wanted me to hit him and

spit on him

melt wax and shit and -

I cut him too

a little

with a razor blade?

that's what he liked

NATHAN: did he

did he do stuff like that to you

MARIE: some yeah

some

pause

NATHAN: was this a thing you did a lot

I mean

was this normal

before him?

MARIE: no

no

no just with him

pause

NATHAN: he hit you

MARIE: in bed, yes

NATHAN: and you liked it

MARIE: I did

    yes

NATHAN: when he hit you?

MARIE: yes

    (pause)

it's just a sensation

    when you're in it

    it's

    it felt like he wanted me

    and it made me want him

    it worked

    I guess

    (pause)

    that really was the only interesting thing about him though

    pause

NATHAN: the next few days I can't stop thinking about it

    imagining what that guy is like

    what that tattoo looked like on his abs

    harder and more sharply defined than mine

    imagining what he and Marie did in bed

    I watched a lot of porn

    to see how it was done

    but that just left me feeling

    more

    defeated

somehow

Nathan and Max

MAX: what's the big deal

NATHAN: I just don't understand it

MAX: it's no big deal

NATHAN: I think I could do it but

I mean look I could DO anything, I COULD do ANYTHING but I just don't have the natural impulse to like WHACK someone while we're

(gesture)

MAX: well you're gonna have to learn then

NATHAN: A bite: yes

a tight squeeze: sure

but to hit someone, I just

MAX: You know what Dan Savage says

NATHAN: I'm not totally "vanilla" I just

when I like someone why would I want to

MAX: "when people are sexually incompatible they gotta break up"

NATHAN: like what, like - if my *T count* was higher I'd be more like that?

MAX: it's not a hostile act when the other person wants it

you gotta stop thinking about it as a hostile act

it's just like she said

it's just a sensation

NATHAN: no

no

something's wrong

either something's wrong with me or something's wrong

with her, or

MAX: what would be wrong with her

she told you

NATHAN: I dug it out of her

MAX: all I'm saying is you better figure it out man

figure it out now cause otherwise *pfft*: it's over

this isn't me talking I'm just telling you what Dan Savage says

pause

MAX: do you like her

NATHAN: yes I like her

MAX: and you don't want to lose her

NATHAN: no

I don't

MAX: well

then you better figure it out

NATHAN: one week later we were at her house

in bed again and things seemed to be going well

in that two and a half months in sweet spot and I thought

it's now

it's now it's now it's –

Hard Cut to:

Nathan and Marie in bed

Marie at one end

Nathan at the other

pause

NATHAN: ...you didn't like it?

MARIE: no

pause

NATHAN: but I thought

MARIE: why did you do that?

NATHAN: I thought that's what you wanted

    I thought that's what you like

MARIE: why would you think that

NATHAN: you told me

    you told me that whole story

    that guy

    the scum tattoo

    you seemed into it and

    I wanted to show you I'm like

    progressive, I can adapt

    I'm not some like

    sexual dinosaur

    (long pause)

    I did it because I like you, Marie

    pause

MARIE: *(not looking at him)*

    I did like it

    with him

    I did that with *him*

    not with you

    pause

NATHAN: is what she says

    Marie stand up and puts clothes on

NATHAN: a couple weeks later

    I see her at Zendo which is this hipster coffee shop downtown

    and we each order coffee

we make eye contact briefly

but neither one of us says hello

Marie gets dressed

looks at Nathan

he looks at Marie

she exits

NATHAN: a few weeks after that I see her at a show at Launchpad

she's with some guy

he looks dumb

guy appears with Marie loud music indicated

MARIE: *(over music)*

hey

NATHAN: *(over music)*

hey

MARIE: how's it going

NATHAN: ok

you know

MARIE: this is Colin

NATHAN: hi

COLIN: hey

handshake

pause

MARIE: I'm gonna

go get a drink

(to Nathan)

do you want any //

COLIN: will you get me a Maker's?

MARIE: oh

yeah

be right back

Marie exits

pause

the men watch the band

COLIN: you like this

NATHAN: what

COLIN: the - ?

(gestures "band" "music")

NATHAN: oh yeah

they're cool

I

I've seen 'em like a dozen times, so

COLIN: yeah they're pretty old

still sound ok though

pause

NATHAN: after Marie comes back they kind of scuttle to the side of the club

I watch them a little

trying not to let them see me

towards the end of the night Marie is alone

that guy she's with is in the pit

I watch him

long skinny limbs pushing out into the other bodies

sweating

full of furious energy

a kind of

fearless abandon

like watching volcanos erupt

through a telescope

on the surface of some far off alien planet

during the last song his t-shirt comes up

skinny hairless chest, ribs and abs protruding like a teenage boy's

down on his belly

in a tight calligraphic font

I see the word "scum" is written

in bold

black

letters

pause

Marie watches Colin

Nathan looks at Marie

End of play.

GLAD FOR THE COMPANY

By Tucker Rafferty

Inspired by "Nebraska" by Bruce Springsteen

CHARACTER

> CHARLIE: Mid to late twenties. Good looking. He's glad for the company.

SETTING

> The entire action of the play takes place in a prison storeroom. Boxes are stacked. There is a cheap fold up cot in the corner. A metal folding chair sits next to the cot. A box is used as a dinner tray. On the dinner tray is a fried chicken dinner complete with biscuits, mashed potatoes and gravy. There is an overflowing ashtray sitting next to the dinner plate.

TIME

> Summer 1959

*The entire action of the play takes place in an aban-
doned prison store room. There are boxes stacked all
around. A cot is center with no blankets or pillow, just
a mattress. A box has been put beside the cot to act
as a make shift table and night stand. On the table is
a bucket of chicken, mashed potatoes, coleslaw, and
empty bottles of coke. On the mattress is a carton of
Camel cigarettes, an overflowing ashtray and a note-
book. Charlie sits on the bed smoking.*

CHARLIE: Another Preacher man comin' to see me. Third one
this week. They told me you were comin'. I don't have a
lot to say. Don't get me wrong, I'm glad for the company,
but I don't have a lot to say. This place can make you feel as
lonesome as a coyote. That's the worst of it nobody to talk
to. Cigarette? I've been smokin' since they brought me into
this closet. They brought me a whole carton. I figured I ain't
gonna let 'em go to waste, right? I asked for Lucky's and they
brought me Camel's. I'd even smoke Chesterfields before
I'd smoke a Camel, but beggars can't be choosers, right? I
wouldn't walk a mile for a Camel, that's for sure.

(Offers cigarette)

You sure?

(Pause)

No skin off my nose.

*(Lights a cigarette for himself and spins lighter be-
tween fingers)*

My daddy taught me that trick.

(Spins lighter again)

Only thing he ever taught me.

(Spins lighter again)

But he taught me good.

(Spins lighter again)

He used to smoke Chesterfields. Got me going, smokin' 'em. Chesterfields. There was a slogan, right? "Chesterfields satisfy."

(Uses sexy voice)

Sexy like, right? Satisfy.

(Laughs)

Satisfy. Cool, right?

(Spins lighter again)

The old man never thought I'd amount to much. "Be glad they need someone to collect other people's garbage" he'd say. We never really did see eye to eye. It got to a point that I'd ignore him or stay out till I thought he'd gone to bed. Some nights he'd sit in the dark and wait for me to kick my shoes off and then he'd say: "You keep standin' on that corner garbage man's gonna collect you."

(Slight pause)

I guess I got the last laugh on him, huh? Newspaper reporters, photographers…there's even some lawyer talkin' to the Supreme Court of these United States on my behalf. Heck, one of the guards wanted to know if I'd sign my name on my old wash rag. Another one wants this here lighter you know, after. Hell, you're here listening to me talk aren't you? Yesiree, I got the last laugh on the old man, huh?

(Pause)

Like I said I don't have a lot to say. But I'm glad for the company. They keep you cooped up twenty-three hours a day. Then you get to walk around the yard for an hour. Guards'll pass time with you for that hour but nothing much is ever said. In your cell at least you know there's a person next to you. It doesn't make you feel so alone just knowin' someone's there. Can't talk or guards'll…you know. Tell you what, there's some lonesome hours during the day. Just you and your thoughts. Nothin' worse you can do to a man than leave him alone with his thoughts. Thoughts can haunt you more than any old ghost ever could. I've never been any good at being alone. Sometimes you get so lonesome—

(Stops abruptly)

The worst thing you can do to a man is leave him alone with his thoughts.

(Pause)

Another Preacher man came to see me last week. He talked more than you do. He told me that my soul would be hurled into a great void. What the heck does that mean? A great void. Does that mean I'm spendin' all of eternity alone? He said Hell is what you make it. If it's hell for you to be alone than it's alone you will be. I don't think I believe that. Do you? I was sorta hopin' for some company.

(Pause)

Piece of chicken? They brought me a whole bucket. I got biscuits and honey here, mashed potatoes, coleslaw a whole Sunday dinner right here. I'm a leg man. Don't get me wrong I like breasts too. And thighs.

(Giggles)

Sorry. I was just foolin' around. You want some chicken? You can have anything you want except the Coke. I've been dying for a Coca-cola.

(Pause)

I'm gonna drink every last one of them. I'm real glad they brought Coke. I don't think I could've choked down a Pepsi.

(Pause)

You lookin' at my cue ball? Shaved it all right off, they did. Looks silly doesn't it? Shaved my arms, arm pits and legs too, can you believe that. They even shaved, you know, down there.

(Pause)

Carol Ann would laugh her pretty head off over this. She used to say I had the most handsome head of hair. That's a funny way of sayin' it, right? Handsome head of hair.

(He laughs)

She said it reminded her of James Dean. Can you imagine that she's comparing me to James Dean. Funny ain't it? She'd say funny stuff like that all the time. Make me laugh. I like him though. James Dean. That red coat he wore. Loved that movie. Saw it a hundred times. Carol Ann's prettier than what's her name?The girl in the movie?…uh Natalie Wood.

(A very good memory, much different tone. Almost dreamily)

First time I ever saw Carol Ann she was standin' right in her daddy's front lawn.She was wearing these dark green shorts and this light green top. She was standin' there. Not so much standin' but posed, yeah posed like a statue made of stone. Then shazam she started twirlin' this baton and spinnin' all over the yard doin' cart wheels and twists. She looked like a grasshopper jumpin' from blade of grass to blade of grass. And then she throws it way up in the air as high as the trees and then she catches it. She catches the thing and falls right into the splits. Most amazing thing I'd ever seen. I knew right then she was the one for me.

(Pause)

Boy oh boy we had us some fun.

(Tone change)

Do you think she'll be here tonight? Probably not, right? If I could have my way I'd have her climb right up on my lap and let 'em strap us in together.

(Pause)

I guess I got lots to say. Just not what you want me to say. I can't and I won't say I'm sorry. No offense to you. I'm glad for your company. But if I say I'm sorry for doin' what we did that would be a lie and I'm a lot of things; a stone cold killer but I'm no liar. That time we spent together was the best time I ever had in my whole life. It was just me and her and nothing much else mattered.

(Pause)

People tried to stop us. People got in the way. Those people died.

(Pause)

Maybe five or six years ago I would tell you that I was sorry for killin' those people. But not anymore and not today. See, it was about then that I realized the Bible was about killin' not salvation. Yeah, I know the Bible. Surprised a guy like me knows about the Bible? Eight years of Sunday school.

(Pause)

You look at it: Cain and Abel, The Great Flood, Sodom and Gomorrah. Killin' Killin' Killin'. Not to mention the dirty tricks he played on Abraham and Job. Cruel.

(Pause)

You see God put it in all of us. Meanness. And we inherited it from God himself. Some of us are really good at denying the meanness, others aren't as good. Look at yourself: a fine upstanding citizen, pay your bills, proud parent, go to church once on Wednesday and twice on Sunday a good God fearing man. But it's in you. You just got it all covered up with all the good you do. But someday it's gonna come seepin' out.

(Pause)

The difference between you and me is you're a God fearing man and me, I live in His image. I hope I get to meet Him tonight. I hope He looks me right in the eye and tells me I can't enter His Kingdom because I killed people. Because then I'm gonna shake His hand, look Him in the eye and say "So did you."

(Silence. Implied visitor exits)

I'm sorry I couldn't accommodate you. Thanks for comin' I really am glad for your company.

(He sits on his cot, lights a cigarette. Takes a long swig of Coke. Long silence.)

Hello out there. Hey. Is anybody out there. I'd be glad for some company.

Blackout.

End of play.

Spirit of Transportation

By Dipika Guha

Inspired by "Streets of Philadelphia" by Bruce Springsteen

CHARACTERS

HENRY: 60's-70's, American, a father.

BEN: 20's, American, his son.

SETTING

30th Street Station, Philadelphia.

Notes on performance:

/ stands for an overlap or an interruption in the dialogue by the next character who speaks

ONE.

We're in Philadelphia's 30th Street Station.

It's a high ceilinged, tall windowed grand old art deco room which ought to create light.

Instead it creates shadows.

People come careening by. We see them only as shadows, moving across the floors, the walls, perhaps the occasional shriek of a train offstage.

Two men, one older, one much younger, sit in a long pew.

The older man wears cowboy boots, sports long sideburns and a plaid shirt and jeans.

He looks weatherbeaten. His eyes are cloudy.

The younger is excruciatingly thin. He's in his twenties but looks younger. He wears jeans and a white t shirt that fall off him. His left knee bounces.

HENRY: It's like uh

BEN: Yeah...

HENRY: Like church!

BEN: Yeah?

HENRY: Yeah!

BEN: Huh.

HENRY: Is it uh...Here?

BEN: The uh....

HENRY: Yeah!

BEN: Yeah, think so.

HENRY: Good! Where?

BEN: It's uh. It's near the rest rooms I think?

HENRY: Near the *rest rooms*?

BEN: Yeah...

HENRY: They put *The Spirit of Transportation,* one of this great country's, no this goddamn world's most famous pieces of art near the restrooms?

BEN: Think so, yeah.

HENRY: This is why this country's goin' down the shitter.

BEN: Literally!

HENRY: Hah! ...

...

Can we go see it?

BEN: I know, uh, you've been looking forward to it.

HENRY: How did you know?

BEN: Last time you called...

HENRY: Right.

BEN: Four years ago.

HENRY: Not that long....

BEN: Yeah it was... you said, "Is it Philadelphia you're living at?"

And I was like, 'Yup'

And you were like... "Is that where the 'Spirit of Transportation' is?"

HENRY: I did not ask you that!

BEN: Yeah you did! Before you know, you asked me/ anything else...

HENRY: (*semi-remorseful*) It's true I have spent a lot of time.... imagining it.

BEN: Yeah?

HENRY: The way the horses just leap right out of the marble.

BEN: Hah..

HENRY: You can practically smell 'em.

BEN: Huh.

HENRY: Nostrils flaring.

Oh boy.

That is a vision!

And boy do we need a vision now.

BEN: We do?

HENRY: This country was made from a vision.

Least...the country I know...the country I seek...

Christ! I bet people don't even see it!

BEN: Well when you gotta go...

HENRY: ....eyes on their cell /phones...

BEN: Well that's a different....

HENRY: Thumbs going crazy...People walking around like shadows, dead to themselves. Don't

look up to see...

BEN sniffs. HENRY gives him a look.

BEN: So, is it uh...is it nice there?

HENRY: Yeah!

Sent you a picture.

BEN: Yeah.

Hills and a river.

Blue skies.

HENRY: It's nice.

BEN: Did you uh...feel like you were, you know...

HENRY: What?

BEN: I don't know...you said you wanted to

....find yourself or something.

HENRY: I did not say that!

BEN: Yeah you did! Nevermind-

HENRY: Well, if you really wanna know, I did. I did find something. Didn't know if I would.

But I got out there and I uh, I felt something good. Something true. Something deep down in this land, I'll tell you. Out there, and oh it's corny to say, but what the hell...I became a a

BEN: A what?

HENRY: A patriot.

BEN sniffs again.

HENRY: How's your uh health?

BEN: Hm?

HENRY: With your uh health?

BEN: Oh.

Same.

HENRY: You're uh..okay now?

BEN: ....yeah...

HENRY: They got good drugs...now huh?

BEN: Yeah.

HENRY: Expensive?

BEN: Not like before.

HENRY: You got that...that new plan?

BEN: Yeah...they cover uh pre-existing uhm conditions so it's uh

A lot cheaper than uh

HENRY: Good, that's good, I haven't heard anything good about that plan so...

That's good...

Are they....they workin' out?

BEN: Yeah. Think so.

I'm still here.

Ha ha!

HENRY: Ha ha! That's good. Good.

BEN: Yeah...

HENRY: Yeah so you're...okay?

BEN: Not getting better.

But not getting worse, you know so...

HENRY: Your mother...she, she did good...looking after you when you uh...

BEN: Yeah she did. I mean...she was/there for me

HENRY: *(tearing up)* You know uh...when you were...

BEN: Oh no...please don't.

HENRY: I should've, I should've, there's uh, I should've uh

BEN: It's /okay....

HENRY: ...Probably uh....

BEN: Naah you, you don't ...

HENRY: No, wait uh I, I, I, I, I do, I uh....

He clutches his heart.

BEN: Oh.

HENRY: You...

Oh. Boy.

This is. Uh. Boy.

You..uh

If a man can't...

BEN: You don't /have to to...

HENRY: I just....you must know. It was uh a hard time for me, for me, too when you uh

BEN: No I I know about that. You were uh struggling. Financially.

HENRY: Didn't uh have the means to, you know, even though I uh

BEN: I know...living out there, wasn't like you could've just uh got on a train!

HENRY: Country isn't built for…we got roads but not

BEN: Trains.

A moment. They stare at each other. HENRY's leg is now bouncing up and down.

HENRY: Shall we?

They stand up. In front of them is now Karl Bitter's marbeled carving "The Spirit of Transportation." We can't see it.

HENRY: They're going, they're going, they're going! They're off! Whooosh!

That's what it's about! Now that's something!

BEN: You keep horses out there, where you live?

HENRY: Yeah! But they don't look like that…look at that mane….

And look over there!

BEN: What?

HENRY: That…

BEN: The baby holding the aircraft?

HENRY: The whole thing…it's a vision….of the future. It's what we need son. We got our land.

That's always gonna be there. But we need something…ya know, bigger to to

BEN: Uh..

HENRY: Unite us.

BEN: So uh..

Is it gonna do the job? Of uniting us?

HENRY: This? I don't know. But it sure as hell is magnificent.

BEN: What if…aw jeez…

HENRY: What? Say it.

BEN: What if we don't need something bigger than, you know *(gives up)*...I don't know.

HENRY: What?

BEN: It's just. It didn't save me okay? When I was really sick... The marble. The horses. The land. It didn't help me.

HENRY: No it was the hospitals, the doctors, the drugs, I know that.

BEN: It was Mom.

But she wasn't who I wanted.

She knew that.

Wasn't easy for her.

But she knew.

That's her though.

Living with what hurts her.

She's got really good at it.

Especially when you left.

I guess some people have more of a chance to practice than others.

HENRY: Didn't wanna tell you straight off.

But my eyesight isn't what it was.

BEN: What?

HENRY: I can't see Ben.

BEN: Are you serious? Well then what are we, what is this...

HENRY: I just, I...I wanted to show you something, I guess, something that meant something to me.

BEN: Are you lying to me about your eyes?

HENRY: Scouts honor.

BEN: Why didn't you say something?

HENRY: I'm saying something now!

BEN: I just thought you wanted to sit in that pew.

HENRY: Too afraid to get up.

Needed the rest room too an hour ago.

BEN: Well it's not far.

HENRY: Well it must be close because we're standing in front of this thing!

BEN: Jeez Dad.

HENRY: I'm a coward.

BEN: And I've

HENRY: "Give me your hungry, your blind and your sick..." isn't that what she said?

BEN: Uh I don't think so?

HENRY: I spent hours looking at photos of this thing and now I can't even...

Henry tears up.

BEN: Here.

HENRY: What?

BEN: Give me your hands. Give them to me.

BEN takes HENRY's hands. He passes them gently over the sculpture that we can't see.

BEN: These are the hooves.

And that there...that's the baby with the aircraft...

HENRY: You were that baby Ben.

You were full of light.

Transporting me up to the heavens.

HENRY takes BEN's hands.

And for a moment, the shadows are at rest.

Then darkness.

End of play

MERRY-GO-ROUND MAN

By Edward Allan Baker

Inspired by "Cover Me" by Bruce Springsteen

CHARACTERS

  ARCANGELO *(ARC)* O'MALLEY

  BEETLE *(DANNY)* SWEET

PLACE/TIME

  North Providence, R.I./Summer of 2015.

SETTING

  A cluttered basement in the tenement house owned by Beetle
  and Candi Sweet.

PRE-SHOW MUSIC

  Popular Songs of the 80's.

"One Of The Problems Of Life
Is To See Whether It's Possible To Live
Without Sorrow."

J. Krishnamurti

LIGHTS UP ON BEETLE (50ish), a lanky body clad in denim and a baseball cap on backwards, ironing a bowling shirt in a corner of the basement that's been hollowed out from junk saved in boxes making space for a cot, laundry baskets, lawn chairs, suitcases, and a square fan. A row of ironed bowling shirt's hang from a rack. ARC, (50ish), is on the cot. He's a gaunt looking man, casually dressed, a small suitcase at his feet. The men stay quiet for some moments. Only the whir of the fan is heard.

It's nearly mid-afternoon.

ARC: *(Finally)* Look, Beetle, I know all this is, um...

BEETLE: *(Ironing)* Nuts, man. It's fuckin' jack-shit crazy.

ARC: I had to come here.

BEETLE: Shoulda just stayed away.

ARC: I couldn't.

BEETLE: It's been twenty-five years, man.

ARC: I don't have much time.

BEETLE: Yeah, you said.

ARC: I'm done with stuff 'out there.'

BEETLE: Yeah, you said. *(Keeps ironing)*

ARC: Good to see you, though.

BEETLE: Sure.

ARC: I mean it.

BEETLE: Right.

ARC: Look at me, Beetle.

BEETLE: I can hear you.

ARC: No, look at me.

BEETLE: I'm good.

ARC: I fucked up a little, I know.

BEETLE: More than a little.

ARC: I know it's hard for you right now…

BEETLE: And I don't deal with 'hard' too good.

ARC: Me either.

BEETLE: You should leave.

ARC: I have to talk with Candi.

BEETLE: Not a good idea.

ARC: I'm dying, Beetle.

BEETLE: Yeah, you said.

ARC: I have to make something right with her.

BEETLE: Yeah, you said.

ARC: *Then* I'll go.

BEETLE: Should go now.

ARC: *(Rises, goes to Beetle)* Stop ironing for a minute.

BEETLE: It's what I do on Wednesday. I iron the team shirts. *(Beat)* So—back off.

ARC: Okay, okay. *(Returns to the cot)* I'm sorry.

BEETLE: It's my routine. Thursday, I food shop.

ARC: Uh-huh.

BEETLE: Friday, I clean the bathroom down here and upstairs.

ARC: I don't remember a bathroom being down here.

BEETLE: I put it in.

ARC: Did you go into plumbing for work?

BEETLE: Shit, no. *(Beat)* I took over my old man's business.

ARC: Running the Park Merry-Go-Round?

BEETLE: Yeah. Now I do it.

ARC: You make a living doing that?

BEETLE: I do okay.

ARC: Really?

BEETLE: Combined with sellin' weed I do okay.

ARC: We toked up plenty down here, didn't we?

BEETLE: I also mow the grass at a coupla Veteran cemeteries.

ARC: Fitting. You loved war stuff.

BEETLE: Mostly the Civil War.

ARC: I remember.

BEETLE: I was definitely a Union Soldier.

ARC: What?

BEETLE: Just a strong feelin' I got from a dream once.

ARC: *(Laughs)* How much weed *do* you smoke?

BEETLE: *(Angrily)* Don't fuck with my mind, Arc!

ARC: I'm not.

BEETLE: *(Pointedly)* You have no right to fuck with my mind.

ARC: Sorry, I'm just into saying what I think, and...

BEETLE: *(Cuts him off)* Cause you're dyin', you said.

ARC: Bluntness is one of the perks of dying.

BEETLE: One of the what?

ARC: Perks.

BEETLE: What's that?

ARC: Um, gift?

BEETLE: Don't get what you're sayin'.

ARC: Forget it.

BEETLE: Cause you're dyin'—you get gifts?

ARC: Let's go with that.

BEETLE: Don't fuck with my mind, Arc.

ARC: I'm not, I'm not. Jesus...

BEETLE: *(After a moment)* I'm sorry you're dyin'.

ARC: Yeah, well…*whadda-ya gonna do…*

BEETLE: You wanna get stoned?

ARC: No—but thanks. *(Silence for some moments)* Where does Candi work?

BEETLE: On Monday and Wednesday she's at Cardi's Bakery.

ARC: One on Fruit Hill Avenue?

BEETLE: Where else would Cardi's Bakery be?

ARC: Thought maybe they expanded.

BEETLE: On Tuesday and Thursday she works at Benny's Hardware.

ARC: So, you guys keep busy.

BEETLE: Gotta work our asses off to keep health insurance.

ARC: I hear you. *(Beat)* You have kids?

BEETLE: My parents are our kids.

ARC: Not doing well?

BEETLE: On Sunday's we take them for rides on the merry-go-round.

ARC: That must be fucking weird for your dad, no?

BEETLE: *(Ironing)* Not weird for him. Weird for me, holdin' him the way he held me when I went round-and-round, afraid to let go of the pole.

ARC: That's nice, Beetle.

BEETLE: Job of the son is the way I see it.

ARC: You're a god son.

BEETLE: Fuck you.

ARC: Okay.

BEETLE: I mean it, man.

ARC: I felt it.

BEETLE: You don't feel shit!

ARC: Let's not fight.

BEETLE: We were like brothers.

ARC: Absolutely.

BEETLE: Fuck you "absolutely."

ARC: What? We *were* close.

BEETLE: Then why did you just up and split without tellin' me, huh?

ARC: There's a reason.

BEETLE: Let's hear it.

ARC: I have to tell Candi first.

BEETLE: She hates you—so tell me then I'll tell her.

ARC: That would be the easy way out.

BEETLE: Isn't that your way?

ARC: Not anymore.

BEETLE: It's been twenty-five years, Arc.

ARC: I've changed.

BEETLE: 'Cause of the rocks in your head.

ARC: Not only.

BEETLE: You didn't come back when your mother died or when your father remarried for a minute, then *he* died, but after twenty-five years you pop in on your once best friend—who is now married to the person *you* were engaged to, which will be twenty-five years next month.

ARC: Okay if I say congratulations on that?

BEETLE: Not a lot of easy times.

ARC: I understand.

BEETLE: *(Firmly)* On account of what you did.

ARC: I know, I know…

BEETLE: You left her a note, then fuckin' disappeared.

ARC: *(Solemnly)* It's what I did.

BEETLE: Cold man, really fuckin' cold.

ARC: It was, but...

BEETLE: Like ya died.

ARC: Like I died.

BEETLE: And makin' it worse was that it was right after we buried Candi's Mother.

ARC: I know.

BEETLE: Cold man, really fuckin' cold.

ARC: I had to go.

BEETLE: You had to go.

ARC: I had to.

BEETLE: To Buffalo, you said.

ARC: I lived in Buffalo.

BEETLE: Immensely fucked up, man.

ARC: I agree with all my heart, even *with* a pacemaker.

BEETLE: A ticker problem, too?

ARC: It's kept going with stents and a pacemaker.

BEETLE: Shit, you might croak *before* Candi gets here.

ARC: That's not so far-fetched. *(Pause)* What are you thinking, Beetle?

BEETLE: How you're fuckin' up my Wednesday.

ARC: Sorry. *(Looks at the shirt Beetle's ironing)* So you're into bowling now?

BEETLE: On Saturday nights, we bowl.

ARC: That's nice.

BEETLE: Stop pretendin' like you care what I do. None of what happened woulda happened if you didn't decide one day to not stay around like the rest of us did! *You* should be ironin' Candi's bowlin' shirt instead a me!

ARC: Well, it is what it is, and if I...

BEETLE: *(Cuts him off)* But come to think of it, you were different; aloof with your parents, yunno, never showin' any *real* affection to them or anyone for that matter.

ARC: They were old when they had me! They were, I don't know—just fucking old!

BEETLE: They're your fuckin' parents!

ARC: And they named me *Arcangelo* O'Malley.

BEETLE: Havin' you was special so they picked a special name so fuckin' what!

ARC: You're right, stupid point. But we weren't close, you were around them, you saw.

BEETLE: I saw your embarrassment around 'em. *(Beat)* Don't understand how someone chooses *not* to be close to their parents, 'specially when the parents were as nice and decent as yours.

ARC: *(After a moment)* I did talk to my father a few times over the years.

BEETLE: Pardon me if I don't applaud.

ARC: He told me you married Candi. *(Silence)* What time does she get off work?

BEETLE: Sometimes three, sometimes four.

ARC: Look, I know I messed up your head just showing up, but...

BEETLE: *(Slams down the iron)* She's pounding at my door, sobbing like I never seen a woman sob, and she shows me your scribbled note, uh, "I have to move away from here, from you, have to leave everything behind and I'm so sorry for the pain it's going to cause, I really and truly am. Goodbye."

ARC: *(Head down)* That was bad.

BEETLE: Let me ask you the million-dollar question—you like the boys?

ARC: Christ, no.

BEETLE: It be easier to take if you walked away to live your gay life in a strange place like Buffalo, you know what I'm sayin'?

ARC: I'm not gay.

BEETLE: Too bad, yunno, 'cause people aren't as shocked by that choice anymore.

ARC: Is that what people were saying about me?

BEETLE: "Must be a fag," was brought up, yeah, but not around your Parents.

ARC: Well, not gay, not then, not now. I actually got married up there but it didn't last.

BEETLE: Kids?

ARC: Nope. *(Beat)* Why didn't you guys have any?

BEETLE: Tried. But Candi couldn't hold 'em long enough.

ARC: What does that mean?

BEETLE: Miscarriages, man, miscarriages.

ARC: Oh. Sorry about that. *(Beat)* And I'm sorry you have to see me dying.

BEETLE: Right. *(After a moment)* You look like your father just before he died.

ARC: You were with him?

BEETLE: Yeah. *(Beat)* Held his hand until he took his last breath.

ARC: So, he went peacefully?

BEETLE: What the fuck—whadda you care?

ARC: *(Suddenly)* I care all right?!

BEETLE: *(Goes at Arc)* Don't you dare yell at me in my fuckin' house!

ARC: *(Hands up)* You're right, you're right, I have no right.

BEETLE: *(Fists clenched)* Damn right you have no right!

ARC: I...I just need to talk with Candi, then I plan on crawling under a porch like an injured cat—and die.

BEETLE: I boarded up under my porch 'cause the old man liked to hide there. *(Returns to the ironing board. Silence)* You become a Bills fan?

ARC: Never lost allegiance to the Patriots.

BEETLE: 'Cause if you told me you had...

ARC: You'd kill me before my heart did.

BEETLE: Go Pats.

ARC: Go Pats.

BEETLE: First good thing you said today.

ARC: Fucking Brady, right?

BEETLE: Ay, best of the best.

ARC: And how about the Sox, huh?

BEETLE: Three World Championships, man!

ARC: Big Papi, Pedro, Manny.

BEETLE: Fuck the Yankees!

ARC: Hate the Yankees.

BEETLE: Four straight playoff wins sent 'em home cryin'!

ARC: Fuck the Yankees!

BEETLE: Hate the Yankees!

ARC: That will never go away.

BEETLE: Takin' it to the grave.

ARC: I'm going first.

    Beetle stays fixed on Arc.

BEETLE: So...what you said before 'bout, 'rocks in your head,' um...

ARC: Small tumors.

BEETLE: You feel 'em?

ARC: No. But I will when they get bigger. My memory will start to go.

BEETLE: Can't take 'em out?

ARC: I'm not letting that happen.

BEETLE: You don't wanna live longer?

ARC: No, I don't Beetle, which is why I need to talk with Candi before I start forgetting.

BEETLE: She's gonna flip, don't know if I'm prepared, yunno, I don't handle things that are 'hard' very well.

ARC: How is she?

BEETLE: Well, considerin' she's had to live with the name of Candi *Sweet,* and not Candi *O'Malley,* she's okay. *(Imitation of Candi)* "Candi Sweet sounds like some Stripper from freakin' South Providence!"

ARC: That how she talks now?

BEETLE: Little bit.

ARC: Her health good?

BEETLE: She's diabetic, like every other person around here, but deals with it, like every other person around here.

ARC: Managing.

BEETLE: No choice. *She* wants to live longer.

ARC: That's good.

BEETLE: Drinks Diet Coke like it's water. Eye-sight's goin'.

ARC: Is it serious?

BEETLE: Shit, she might not even recognize you.

ARC: Really, how bad is it?

BEETLE: Can still work and shit but bowlin' scores dropped some; more gutter balls, but no one makes a big deal out of it. Everybody loves Candi.

ARC: She loved to bowl.

BEETLE: Still does but average has dropped some.

ARC: You said.

BEETLE: More gutter balls.

ARC: Uh-huh.

> *Beetle keeps ironing. Arc stares at the wall, lost in thought.*

BEETLE: Do you remember who I was with when you and Candi were goin' out?

ARC: *(Turns to Beetle)* Um, girl from the East Side, pretty blond, different from the neighborhood girls...*um... (Beat)* Joan Morris!

BEETLE: Bingo! After you left the area, Candi leaned quite heavily on me, yunno, for support and comfort *all the time*, right, and Joan just sort of faded away, ended up goin' to Brown, and that's all she wrote. Us Providence Flatlanders can't compete with College Hill girls, even if ya think you can, you can't.

ARC: I never knew it to happen.

BEETLE: You actually told me, right here in this cellar, "she'll never settle on you, Beetle, an East Side girl will never accept the son of The Merry-Go-Round Man."

ARC: Well...I don't remember saying that but it's true.

BEETLE: I gave her the first orgasm she ever had—so she said.

ARC: Well, they don't pretend with the first one so it's probably true.

BEETLE: She wrote me a letter back then tellin' me that my tongue and kisses brought her closer to God.

ARC: *(Laughs)* Get the fuck out of here!

BEETLE: I swear on your Mothers eyes!

ARC: Wow, "closer to God," and she still left you!

BEETLE: I was the son of The Merry-Go-Round Man.

ARC: We're talking feeling 'God' here, had to be more than a class issue, no?

BEETLE: *(Spills out)* She left me because I was spendin' so much of my time with Candi—so she thought that me and her were, yunno, fuckin' on the side!

ARC: Were you?

BEETLE: Of course we were!

ARC: Oh.

BEETLE: For chrissakes, we even did it *on* the merry-go-round to Waltz music.

ARC: Okay, we don't have to get into this.

BEETLE: It was pity screwin', man, no fun on account of you! I wanted Joan!

ARC: I get it, okay, I…

BEETLE: *(Interrupts)* Screwin' Candi…who is sobbin' the whole time, felt like I was committin' a crime when I was tryin' to do good!

ARC: Again, I'm sorry you had to go—

BEETLE: *(Interrupts)* So, marriage happened, right, and one day Candi comes down here, and I look up and she's holdin' the letter Joan wrote me that I *stupidly* saved, and she's wavin' it in my face, then says, "if we're to stay together, I want you to *eat* this letter."

ARC: And did you?

BEETLE: Bet your ass I did! Between two pieces of toast *with* mayo and salt.

ARC: She watch you eat it?

BEETLE: Yeah. She knew *even then* me bein' alone would kill me.

ARC: So you never talked about it?

BEETLE: We're a B-side couple, man, certain inside-issues we don't go to in a deep way. But we're together. *(Beat)* We're together…

ARC: I get it.

BEETLE: Livin' in our routine, smokin' weed, bowlin', watchin' the tube, go to wakes and weddings, bitch about money, and in August we go to the Cape for whale watchin'. We're fine. She boxes pastry, sells nails, and I yell to kids, "hang on to the pole!"

Pause. Beetle irons.

ARC: I remember Candi's dream of wanting to be a cheerleader for the Patriots. *(Beat)* I drove her to her first tryout.

BEETLE: I was with you that day, ya fuck.

ARC: Shit, that's right, you were there.

BEETLE: *With* Joan Morris. A natural fuckin' high that day, and most *North* of Providence I ever was.

ARC: In my Father's sky-blue Ford Galaxy.

BEETLE: Massachusetts breeze comin' through the open windows, Springsteen song blarin',

Joan under my arm. *(Beat)* Could've driven to Canada, I wouldn't a cared.

ARC: Was a fun time.

BEETLE: Little did we know.

ARC: How could we?

BEETLE: That shortly after you'd pick up and run away.

ARC: I wish I could go back.

BEETLE: Did you know then that you'd walk away?

ARC: No.

BEETLE: Did you love Candi back then?

ARC*: (Shrugs)* I…I don't know…um…

BEETLE: Find the truth in-between the rocks, c'mon man…! Did you love…

ARC: *(Suddenly)* Stop, all right! I don't fucking know, so drop it! I need to talk with Candi, that's the only truth I'm thinking about right now, and I apologize for my surprise visit...but dying has driven me here to come clean with Candi!

BEETLE: *(Goes at Arc, lifts him up by his shirt)* Apologize for yellin' at me in my cellar!

ARC: *(Afraid)* Sorry, I'm sorry. *(Stares hard at Beetle)* We were like brothers, did so much together...I missed you in my life more than... *(Beetle holds eye-contact with Arc for a moment before releasing him to fall back on the cot. He returns to the ironing)* I mean it, man...

BEETLE: Heard ya. *(Ironing in silence. Finally)* What did you do for work up there?

ARC: *(Sits up on his elbows)* I was a Counsellor at a school for emotionally disturbed teenage boys. Worked the graveyard shift. Bed checks, and talked them back to sleep after a bad dream.

BEETLE: *(Laughs) You* workin' with emotionally disturbed teen-agers. I gotta tell ya, I find that kinda funny, considerin'...

ARC: Considerin' what?

BEETLE: C'mon man, you had a little bit of a lyin' problem and you liked to steal shit, like sneakin' some of my dope when you could've just asked me for some, and you always used to over exaggerate shit that happened or *didn't* happen.

ARC: I did it a lot?

BEETLE: It's who you were, and nothin' like bein' into violent shit but deep down I didn't really trust *half* of you. *(Beat)* You were...sneaky.

ARC: *(Sits up straight, talking to himself)* A lying thief...a mother fucking lying thief, sneaking around...

Stands, begins to pace, hands covering his face.

BEETLE: *(Looks over at Arc)* You okay there?

ARC: *(Stops, looks at Beetle)* And you...you still stayed my friend...

BEETLE: Forget it, man. *(Beat)* Hey, remember you wanting to be a Radio Dee-Jay?

ARC: *(Distracted)* Yeah, yeah.

BEETLE: You were goin' into broadcastin', me to Johnson and Wales to be a Chef in some fancy joint on The Hill.

ARC: *(Suddenly)* You should've called me out on shit, Beetle! You should've said, "Arc, you're a two-bit liar and thief, and if you don't fucking cut it out I won't be your friend, so clean up your fucking act, and be straight, man! Be fucking honest, mannnnn!" I would've listened to you!

BEETLE: *(Goes to Arc)* Whoa, whoa, cut the shit, hey! Whaddaya doin'?

ARC: You let me be something I didn't *have* to be! Fuck! You should've kicked my ass up and down Manton Avenue!

BEETLE: Listen, Rip Van *Fuckin'* Winkle, friends didn't *fix* friends where we're from! We *accepted* what was in front of us without, "can I tell you what I *really* think about you?"

ARC: *(Collapses on the cot)* You...oh my freaking god...*you* might've made a difference!

BEETLE: What the fuck are you talkin' about? You're makin' this about *me*?!

ARC: You knew I was this...this...petty lying jerk who wasn't to be trusted...and you...

BEETLE: *(He grabs Arc by the arm)* I want you out, really Bro, you gotta split...!

ARC: *(Looks up at Beetle, his face twisted in agony)* I...I...

He breaks free of Beetles grasp, pushes some boxes and junk away from a wall, then loosens a wooden panel and in one quick move rips it off the wall.

BEETLE: What the fuck are you doin'?!

Arc reaches down into the exposed opening and pulls out a black gym bag that he tosses to Beetle.

ARC: Open it! *(Beetle stares down at the bag)* Open it!

Beetle unzips the bag and takes out a woman's pocketbook. He looks up at Arc, confused.

ARC: It's Candi's Mother's pocketbook…

BEETLE: What?

ARC: I took it from the back of a chair left at Iggy's restaurant. I didn't know whose it was at the time…I just shoved it in my gym bag, you know, came here thinking I would splitwhatever was there with you; took out the cash, about forty bucks, never looking to see whose it was…then stashed it in the wall.

BEETLE: *(Opens up the pocketbook, pulls out the wallet, checks a photo)* Jesus fuckin' Christ…

ARC: That night I got a hysterical Candi on the phone telling me her Mother died, her…her fucking mother died because *she lost her pocketbook* and didn't have… *(He takes the pocketbook from Beetle, and pulls a vial of pills from the handbag)* her heart pills...

BEETLE: *(In one quick move, Beetle has Arc around the throat)* I should make you eat these fuckin' pills! *(After a moment of choking Arc, Beetle drops his hands)*

ARC: *(Scurries to a corner, gasping for air)* I…I couldn't see Candi or go to the wake, how could I?! So, with the stolen cash, I bought a bus ticket to go as far North as forty bucks would take me.

BEETLE: *(Stares hard at Arc)* You piece a shit…

ARC: My punishment was living a miserable life for twenty-five years and now I…I…

BEETLE: Shut up! *(Pacing, angrily)* I gotta think so shut the fuck up!

ARC: *(Steps to Beetle)* I have to come clean to Candi… *(Goes to the cot. Sits)*

BEETLE: *(Moves to the cot, stands over Arc)* No, no you don't! You'll do nothing like that, you understand me, mother-fucker?! *(Beat)* Do you?!

ARC: Beetle… *(Tries to sit up but Beetle pushes him back down)*

BEETLE: Candi can't find out you killed her mother because if she finds out what you did, she'll sink into some dark place, a place far away from me that I'll have to deal with, and I don't want that for her, and I don't that for me! *(Leans down)* Is this gettin' through the rocks in your head?!

ARC: I…I must talk with her…please…let me…

BEETLE: *(In Arc's face, controlling his anger)* Oh, you can talk with her but it's goin' to be about askin' for forgiveness for breakin her heart and leavin' her, and that's it! You tell her that…I don't know…her sudden outta control *neediness* freaked you the fuck out so you bolted—or, better yet, tell her you were about to reveal that you're gay, then her mother died, so you went North; I don't give a shit, but know this former best friend, I'm not goin' to let you hurt her again; not gonna jeopardize the life we have made for ourselves, okay? We're decent people tryin' to do what we can with what we have, and this past mistake you've brought to this house will not affect what little of the future we have left! *(After a moment of staring down at Arc, he rises from the cot, swipes up the handbag, shoves it back into the wall, fits back the panel, then kicks back boxes against the wall. He pauses, turns to Arc)* You stashed the pocketbook in my house even after knowing what you had done. Jesus Christ, man…

ARC: *(Barely audible)* I got scared…

> Beetle takes the vial of pills and goes to the bathroom
> to flush the pills down. Arc is on his back staring up
> at the ceiling. Beetle re-enters the space and smashes
> the vial with his foot—then drops the pieces in a box
> marked, "for the dump."

BEETLE: Here's the deal Candi gave me that I'm now givin' you:

91

do what I ask, and I'll make sure you don't die alone—which I don't think you really want to do.

ARC: *(After a moment)* No.

BEETLE: Don't fuck us over *twice*, Arc…

ARC: *(Softly)* I'll do what you asked.

BEETLE: That the truth? *(Arc holds out his hand. Beetle takes it)*

ARC: *(Tiredly)* The truth… *(Candi is heard upstairs. The men go silent to listen)*

BEETLE: She's home. *(Beat)* You're goin' to lie one more time. *(Beat)* Your last lie.

ARC: *(Nods)* Okay.

Beetle heads up the stairs and after a moment the muffled voice of Beetle talking to Candi is heard. Arc opens his suitcase to remove a clean shirt. He stands to remove the shirt he has on revealing his bare chest spotted with black and blue bruises, a few surgical scars, a rash around the protruding pacemaker.

CANDI: *(Cheerfully, from upstairs)* Oh my god, Arcangelo O'Malley, you get up here, let me see ya!

Arc looks up, afraid, and half alive—he stands motionless.

BLACKOUT.

End of play.

THE STRAY

By Scott T. Barsotti

Inspired by "Highway Patrolman" by Bruce Springsteen

CHARACTERS

> JOE ROBERTS: Under 40, FRANK's older brother and MARIA's boyfriend. Also chief of police.
>
> FRANK ROBERTS: Under 40, JOE's younger brother.
>
> MARIA: similar age to JOE, JOE's girlfriend.
>
> DENICE FAIR: a living ghost.
>
> SARAH BRADLEY: a ghost.
>
> BILL MAYNOR: a ghost.
>
> Additional "Ghosts of Frank's Wreckage," as desired.

SETTING

> A small post-industrial town in the U.S., and the surrounding highways.

TIME

> Any time after the mills closed.

Dark stage. A flashlight clicks on, illuminating MA-RIA. FRANK ROBERTS comes up to her. She doesn't really react to him. He brazenly grabs her breast, not really in a sexual way, in a sort of "Hey, I'm gonna grab that" kinda way. He keeps his hand there, doesn't stop, doesn't look her in the eyes, just keeps rubbing. She looks down in shock, her mouth hangs open. She looks at Frank.

MARIA: Um...

FRANK: Yep.

She's too appalled to do anything, just stands there, revolted.

MARIA: Oh my god.

FRANK: Oh my god.

MARIA: Um...

FRANK: 'Oh my god' she says.

MARIA: Do you mind?

FRANK: I don't mind.

MARIA: What are you doing?

FRANK: Fact-finding.

MARIA: (*laughs despite herself, disgusted.*) Would you get your hands off me?

He does.

FRANK: Took you long enough.

MARIA: Fuckin' Frank.

The flashlight clicks off. Darkness. A flashlight clicks on, illuminating JOE ROBERTS. He is not holding the flashlight, it comes from elsewhere.

JOE: I see the faces of his wreckage. What he left behind. I see them in my dreams. In the corners of my eyes. They hang above me, looking at me. Looking. They never speak. I don't know what they want from me. I didn't protect them, I know. But...nothing I can do about it now. I didn't protect them, and I don't get another chance.

Joe clicks on his flashlight and shines it on Frank. Frank holds the flashlight shining on Joe. Frank clicks his flashlight off. This exchange happens throughout.

FRANK: I'm sittin' at the bar, whiskey in my hand, sweating, pissed off the Jets and Devils both lost, had money on both, no surprise. No surprise. I always bet on losers.

JOE: They never speak but...I hear them. Like they're in my brain, speaking against the insides of my ears. No. Not speaking. Breathing.

An exhale, he turns and shines his light. He turns back.

JOE: They don't tell me anything. They only remind me.

FRANK: Had plenty to drink, I've always had plenty to drink. Tellin' stories that some people in the bar don't like to hear. That's what I do. Say that shit. Can't stop me, everyone wants to stop me, no one does. One asshole can ruin everyone's lives. I am well aware. And so are they. Afraid of what I'll do if they say somethin'. Right they are.

JOE: Frankie always made a fool out of me. An honest man except where it came to him. Did what I could to look away, but in a town this size, it's no secret you're playing favorites. Everyone knew. At first my inaction was met with bewilderment. Then outrage. Then eventually...apathy.

FRANK: I never planned to live past 40. I'm everybody's least favorite kind of person.

JOE: They stopped caring...stopped thinking it mattered to care. Stopped asking for help. (*Joe's light shines around*) They'd just look at me.

FRANK: Everything would be fine if nobody would talk to me. It's voices. Every human voice is a shrill, piercing whine to me. It all sounds like misery, can't have a girlfriend with that going on. Maria maybe. She's the only one. Even then.

JOE: I always thought ghosts were dead. Always believed that. But these faces...sometimes they're of people still...around. They come to avenge my neglect. My lenience on Frank. But it's just visions. And breath. One minute I see them. The next...(*shines his light.*) Nothing. No eyes. No judgment. Only me.

FRANK: Joey always knew I had a thing for Maria. Made him uncomfortable. Made him *really*...uncomfortable. He'd catch me lookin' at her. Kissin' her on the cheek but you know, half on the lips. Givin' her hugs that lasted too long. But he's just like those do-nothings in the bar. Afraid of what I'll do. Hopin' I'll go away, hopin' I'll just stop of my own accord. Or maybe drop dead.

JOE: This is when I see them the most, when I come out here. By myself. This stretch of road. This is when they approach me. The beaten. The abandoned. The aggrieved. I've been blamed, blamed for it all. You took the good blood. Frank's not good like you.

FRANK: He's too polite. He'll let me get away with anything. I wouldn't say I abuse that though. I just like to get what I can.

JOE: You gotta straighten him out, you're good, your family's good, you can do that. Lean into him a little, he respects you. He doesn't respect me, does whatever he can to embarrass me, undermine me. You gotta keep an eye on him, Joe, like he's a child. You gotta control him, like he's an animal. Keep an eye on your kid, sir. Control your dog, mister.

FRANK: I don't know why anybody expects any more of me than that. I expect very little out of people. I don't see what point there is in havin' any expectations. More than I can count on two hands is how many times I nearly been killed. Step out of an intersection just as a bus goes barrelin' through like its brakes are out. Bullet goes screamin' past my ear, two inches this way it's in my eye. Shit's random. I should be dead. Maybe I am. I probably deserve it.

JOE: Was there a sound? Or am I the only one? Am I the...I can… (*exhales loudly*) They're here. They're around me. (*shines the light, finds a dark, bruised face*) Watching me. They just stare. Like this. Sarah Bradley. She...she killed herself when Frank left her. I couldn't help her. And Frank couldn't let her be...harassed her. Sabotaged her. One night she called me but I... (*shines the light elsewhere, another face*) Bill Maynor...an accident at the plant, might've been Frank's fault. No one ever knew. Frank never said a word. People had suspicions. Not that Frank cared about any of that how could he not care? Bill's here. Watching me. But...Denice Fair. (*another face*) Denice is still alive. Still alive but she's out here haunting me. And she's right to. She's right to. (*he lowers his flashlight*) I don't know what they're gonna do. I just want them to do something. Say something!! (*the faces are gone*) They want me to do something about Frank. That's what it is. They want me to go after him. Go after Frank. They won't let me forget. They won't let me be glad for the peace. They want me to do my job.

Maria approaches Frank

FRANK: Maria walks in and the place is hers. She knows it. Everyone knows it. Nobody says a off word to Maria cause they know she's Joe's. Nobody gets in her way. Nobody but me. Maria don't like me much.

MARIA: Just cause I'm with Joe don't mean I gotta like you, Frank.

FRANK: You're wrong. It means you gotta like me even more.

MARIA: I don't owe you anything.

FRANK: That right?

MARIA: No one owes you anything. Not even Joe. Especially not Joe.

FRANK: I doubt Joey sees it that way, sweetie.

JOE: I can't stop coming out here. It's a compulsion I guess.

MARIA: You should treat your family the best. Instead, people like you assume they'll accept the worst.

FRANK: With a smile.

JOE: Some nights I'm just out driving, I find myself here, without even meaning to, like all roads lead to this spot. I get out of the car, I stare and I listen. Sometimes I sit on the hood. I listen. I get the flashlight. I click it on. (*shines the flashlight, no one there*) Sometimes they're not there. (*he shines it in a different spot, DENICE FAIR is there*) Sometimes they are. I need them to tell me what they want. What I should do. There's a reason they come to me like this, and out here, this place, and it's all sorts that come, it's not just Denice Fair, not just Sarah Bradley. Like I said...it's his wreckage, and his wreckage cuts a wide path. Some nights, there are dozens of faces in the dark. But whether there's twenty of them or just one, they tell me just as much. (*he shines the light on Denice again, and her face has changed, her mouth is open like she wants to speak, but she makes no noise*) There comes a point where you can't defend someone anymore, no matter who they are. Tell me what to do, Denice.

FRANK: Hey...I see you down there.

Denice interacts with Frank

DENICE: Me?

FRANK: Yeah you. You're...Denice!

DENICE: You're Joe Roberts' brother.

FRANK: Good 'ol Joey.

DENICE: I've heard about you.

FRANK: Nothin' good I'm sure.

DENICE: No actually.

FRANK: No actually it was good or no actually it wasn't?

Frank goes to touch her face. She slaps his hand away, turns her back.

JOE: Don't turn your back on me, Frankie.

FRANK: Don't turn your back on me.

JOE: Disgrace our family, our name, you shit on the town's opinion of me. That's turnin' your back.

FRANK: That's not polite, turn your back on a guy.

Denice turns back, she has a bloody nose. She runs from him. Joe catches her in the beam of his flashlight and she freezes, now a ghost on his highway.

JOE: Maria saw what Frank did to Denice Fair.

FRANK: Maria got in my face, thinkin' she's allowed, cause of Joe. I told Maria, all people have to do is ask for what they want, ask for what they don't want, but everyone pussyfoots, everyone's too polite. (*to Maria*) Fuck 'em if they are, ain't my problem.

MARIA: She did nothing to you.

FRANK: Exactly, she didn't ask for shit, was just a bitch and turned her back when I was tryin' to be nice.

MARIA: You weren't tryin' to be nice.

FRANK: How you figure?

MARIA: Cause you ain't nice, Frank!

FRANK: What'd you say?

MARIA: You ain't nice. Ever. There's nothing nice about you and there never has been.

FRANK: And honest...that's no newsflash or anything, but comin' from her. That fucked me up. Next thing I knew Maria was... sorta...between my fingers.

JOE: I come out here, waiting for the night Maria will appear. Waiting for her to guide me. Otherwise I'm lost. I'm no kinda man at all.

FRANK: Her dark skin. Her dark hair. Her blood. Can't even remember what I did. My hands hurt.

JOE: She's a part of his wreckage now. She's one of em who won't ever forgive me.

FRANK: Joey'll be here soon. Which means I shouldn't be.

JOE: I chased him all night. We drove top speed, down the dark highway. We drove for hours.

FRANK: Days.

JOE: Weeks.

FRANK: Months.

JOE: Our gas never ran out.

FRANK: Faster, faster.

JOE: Our tires never gave.

FRANK: He's behind me.

JOE: Our engines never quit.

FRANK: All night. Every night.

JOE: The sun never came up.

FRANK: We just drove and drove.

FRANK/JOE: Always and always.

JOE: Chased him to this road.

FRANK: This spot.

FRANK/JOE: Here.

JOE: Right here.

The Ghosts of Frank's wreckage surround Frank and close in on him.

FRANK: And then I was gone. Gone.

Light out on Frank as the Ghosts grab him.

JOE: I'll never stop comin' here. I know that. Not so long as they're out here. Not so long as Frankie's out there. I didn't save him either. I couldn't. And he haunts me now, too. But I don't see his face. I only see his taillights.

Two flashlights with red beams flank Joe. Light out on Joe, leaving only the taillights for several moments. They click off, leaving quiet darkness.

End of play.

OBJECT PERMANENCE

By Jennifer Blackmer

Inspired by "Terry's Song" by Bruce Springsteen

CHARACTERS

TERRY: Male, 38

MITCH: Male, 30

SETTING

An empty, expansive warehouse somewhere in Cleveland.

Lights up on an empty, expansive old warehouse. TERRY sits in the middle of the floor, shuffling a deck of cards. He is dressed like a carnival barker, sporting a bowler hat, chomping on a cigar. He furls the cards.

TERRY: *(to the empty room)* Pick a card, any card.

He closes his eyes and picks a card out of deck.

TERRY: Don't let me see it.

He places the card face down in front of him, ceremoniously.

TERRY: Okay, now, I'll bet you that I can guess your card!

He shuffles the cards.

TERRY: Tell me when to stop.

MITCH enters, looking like hell. He hasn't slept in days.

MITCH: Stop. *(beat)* And it's the two of clubs. It's always the two of clubs.

TERRY: Not always.

MITCH: It's a rigged deck, Terry. Every other card is the fucking two of clubs.

TERRY: A magician never reveals his secrets.

TERRY holds the card to his forehead.

TERRY: Your card is... the... the... King of hearts.

TERRY flips the card over. It's the two of clubs.

TERRY: You win some. You lose some.

TERRY opens a random old box and removes a bottle of bourbon, and two shot glasses.

TERRY: You want some?

He pours a shot and downs it. MITCH sits on the floor next to him. TERRY pours two shots. They clink glasses.

MITCH: To your health.

TERRY: A little late for that, don't you think?

MITCH: Fuck you.

TERRY: Oh c'mon now! That's funny!!

They drink.

TERRY: What are you doing here, Mitch?

MITCH: Looking for you.

TERRY: I've been to England, France, Iran, Iraq, Kuwait, Dayton, Ohio, Afghanistan, Rio de fuckin' Janeiro. I mean, I saw the Taj Mahal. And you come looking for me in a shitty old warehouse in Cleveland?

MITCH: I found you, didn't I?

TERRY: *(small smile)* Touché.

MITCH: You remember the first time we came here?

TERRY: Remind me.

MITCH: The place had been closed, like a decade, and you and me snuck over the fence and climbed through that window. That one over there. You'd just finished basic, and were getting ready to ship out, so you weren't gonna be home for like, two years—

TERRY: Eighteen months, but go on.

MITCH: Yeah, well it felt like five years, and you had your service pistol and I asked you to teach me how to fire it—

TERRY: Oh, God—

MITCH: And we set up these boxes, and lined up these old glass canisters on top, and you showed me how to aim.

TERRY: You were a natural—

MITCH: And I pulled the trigger and totally fucked it up.

TERRY: You didn't.

MITCH: I hit the goddam window! And then a bunch of the others broke, like some chain reaction or something, and someone called the cops, and they came and we had to run—

TERRY: And you ripped your jeans climbing over the fence—

MITCH: And my tighty whiteys were hanging out for the world to see.

TERRY: You had such a cute butt.

MITCH: And we were running home and we passed Carolyn Letson on the street, and I had the hots for her—

TERRY: SO BAD you had the hots for her—

MITCH: So you thought it'd be a GREAT idea to hang out and talk to her while I'm standing there in my fucking underwear.

TERRY: Yeah, well you guys were together for three years, so you can't blame me for shit. The demise of your relationship was your own doing.

Pause.

TERRY: Tell that story.

MITCH: No.

TERRY: Why not? It'll take me down a few notches.

MITCH: Mom'll kill me.

TERRY: I'm not a saint.

MITCH: Obviously. But she still thinks you are. I'm not gonna take that from her.

Long pause. MITCH pours another drink.

TERRY: Why does it have to be you?

MITCH: Because somebody has to! Mom can't. Cindy sure as hell can't.

TERRY: I'll bet Marquita wants to say something—

MITCH: She does.

TERRY: So let her do it.

MITCH: You'd want that?

TERRY: *(nonchalant)* Sure? Why not?

MITCH: You'd want your overly dramatic second cousin to recite the lyrics to "I'm Proud to be an American" or "Born in the USA" or whatever patriotic shit she thinks the moment deserves?

TERRY: That's cool. I love The Boss.

MITCH: Okay, then. Problem solved.

He starts to go.

TERRY: Wait—

MITCH: What?

TERRY: "Born in the U.S.A." is always taken out of context. You should do my eulogy.

MITCH: So it does matter to you.

TERRY: Of course it matters!! Of course I want you to do my fucking eulogy!

MITCH sits back down.

TERRY: But doesn't you coming here defeat the whole purpose?

MITCH: How?

TERRY: Because it's not about ME. It's about YOU.

MITCH: THAT'S bullshit.

TERRY: People aren't gathering around that hole in the ground to learn something new about me. Hell, kid, between all of them, they know everything anyway, and each one has a different perspective so, in the end, nothing you say is gonna change anyone's mind because they already think what they think, so there. See? Pressure's off.

MITCH: Fuck you.

TERRY: You're my brother. You know me better than anyone.

MITCH: THEN WHY DIDN'T YOU SAY ANYTHING TO ME?? HUH? WHY DIDN'T YOU TELL ME YOU WERE IN TROUBLE?? Jesus God almighty, Terry, I'm just so fucking PISSED OFF at you!!

Small pause.

TERRY: I said you knew me better than anyone, Mitch. I didn't say you knew everything.

MITCH: You were my hero.

TERRY: What does that even MEAN, anyway? Hero? I was a great actor, Mitch. A magician. Nothing up my sleeve—

MITCH: You were an Army Ranger. You served for eighteen years. Three tours in Iraq, one in Afghanistan, and you faced death every single day—

TERRY: Remember Scott Hanney? Guy from my class at school? Riding his bicycle down county road 3 like he does every fucking day, only this one day he's T-boned by a teenager going eighty, and he's thrown into a ditch where he dies instantly. Thirty-eight years old.

MITCH: Yeah, but—

TERRY: Remember Barry Weller? Jerry's older brother? Breaks up with his girlfriend, she moves out, he's living alone for the first time in ten years and he has a fucking heart attack while cleaning his basement. He wasn't even fifty. David Compton, this guy from my unit, was diagnosed with brain cancer on his fortieth birthday and he was dead six months later.

MITCH: Yeah, well, those guys didn't have a choice!

TERRY: And I did?

MITCH: YES! I mean, they expect this kind of thing from the young kids, right? The enlisted men?

TERRY: I was enlisted once.

MITCH: Fucking career Army, Terry. You were supposed to have it figured out!!

TERRY: YEAH, WELL I DIDN'T.

Pause.

TERRY: You know when a kid's a toddler, and everyone plays peekaboo with them?

MITCH: Huh?

TERRY: Peekaboo, asshole. Peekaboo? PEEK-A-FUCKING-BOO. I played it with you!!

TERRY ducks behind a box.

TERRY: Wheeeeeeeere's Terry? Wheeeeere's Terry, huh?

He pops back up.

TERRY: PEEKABOO!

MITCH is not amused.

TERRY: You play peekaboo with the kid so they learn this thing called "object permanence." Right? That when you can't see the thing, it's behind something or around a corner, but it's still there. You can't see it, but it's still there. So the kid learns about object permanence, over and over and over again, until it becomes embedded in their brains, ingrained in their tiny little skulls.

MITCH: Okay. Sure.

TERRY: But that's all a lie, see. The truth is a lie, and the lie is truth. There IS no object permanence.

MITCH: What are you talking about?

TERRY: People DO disappear when they go around a corner, or hide behind a wall. Or go out for morning patrol. Or diffuse an IED. I read somewhere that the human body replaces itself every seven years— every damn cell in my body is new at some point over seven years, so I couldn't have been the same person I was when I enlisted.

MITCH: You're still my brother.

TERRY: Yes I am. And no I'm not. I saved guys from being shot, saved guys from being blown up, I was always watching, watching, waiting for something to happen. And then I come home, and I'm supposed to just turn that all off. Like a switch. Death is supposed to just... happen now, randomly, no explanation, like Scott, like Barry. And there's not a damn thing I can do about it.

MITCH: You didn't have to kill yourself.

TERRY: Yeah, well. I did.

Pause.

MITCH: What did it feel like?

TERRY: What?

MITCH: When you pulled the trigger?

TERRY: Like breathing. I was choking for air, and it was the deepest breath I've ever taken.

Pause.

MITCH: Yeah, well I still don't know what the hell I'm going to say.

TERRY: You'll think of something.

MITCH: They broke the mold.

TERRY: Excuse me?

MITCH: Gramma Pike used to say it about you— "They broke the mold when they built Terry."

TERRY: Yeah. I remember that.

MITCH: It's true. I don't know what I'm going to do without you.

TERRY: Love always cheats death. And it always wins. Even if the deck is rigged.

He fans the cards.

TERRY: Pick a card, brother. Any card.

Blackout.

End of play.

Gospel Hour

By Dan Caffrey and Drew Caffrey

Inspired by "State Trooper" by Bruce Springsteen

CHARACTERS

JAMES: a New Jersey State Trooper, mid-20s.

GRACE: James' wife, heard through his CB radio.

CAROLYN: another voice heard through the radio.

SETTING

James' police cruiser, sometime in 1982.

Darkness. Radio static mixed with various transmissions.

JAMES: *(in darkness)* Grace? I think I lost you.

Lights up on JAMES sitting in a police cruiser parked on the side of a turnpike. He wears a New Jersey State Police uniform. Rain falls outside. The sound of windshield wipers. James looks out the window and speaks into the hand-piece of a CB radio. It's 1982.

JAMES: Grace.

He turns his attention away from the window and fiddles with the CB. More static. A woman's voice breaks through.

GRACE: *(on radio)* James...James?

JAMES: I'm here.

Static.

JAMES: Can you hear me?

Static.

GRACE: Yes.

The static clears. Windshield wipers.

GRACE: Could we go one night without talking on this thing?

JAMES: I like the way you sound on it.

GRACE: You could go to a payphone.

JAMES: It's raining.

GRACE: Sunny over here.

JAMES: It's nighttime, sweetie.

GRACE: Clear outside's what I mean. No water. Just the moon. "Moony."

JAMES: Name of my old track coach.

GRACE: I never had him.

JAMES: Coach Ian Mooney. Moony with an "e." He was only

at Burlington City for a little while. Got fired for sleeping with a student.

GRACE: That happened a lot back then.

JAMES: Still does.

GRACE: People didn't talk about it as much. But I heard about it more.

JAMES: Makes sense. The type of teachers we had.

Pause. Windshield wipers.

GRACE: You near the radio towers?

JAMES: Staring right at them.

GRACE: No speeders?

JAMES: Just me and the towers. Reminds me of *War of the Worlds*. One day they'll come to life.

GRACE: When I was little, I thought they were oil wells. That always scared me.

JAMES: Yeah.

Pause. Windshield wipers.

GRACE: You sound so far away on this thing.

JAMES: I know.

GRACE: Is that why you like talking on it?

Pause. Windshield wipers.

GRACE: Did you talk to her?

JAMES: I did.

GRACE: How'd she take it?

JAMES: How would you take it?

GRACE: Don't do that.

JAMES: What.

GRACE: Compare me to her.

Pause. Windshield wipers.

JAMES: It's over.

GRACE: I know.

JAMES: You believe me this time?

GRACE: There's something in your voice now. I can tell when you're done with things.

JAMES: I didn't want to talk about this tonight.

GRACE: We talked about radio towers.

JAMES: I said I would end it and I did. I don't know what else you want.

Pause. Windshield wipers.

GRACE: Okay.

A baby cries over the CB. James smiles.

JAMES: How's he doing?

GRACE: He has a hard time sleeping when you're gone.

JAMES: Tell him I'm on my way.

GRACE: You're still working.

JAMES: From now on, I'm always on my way. Whatever I'm doing, wherever I am, I'm always coming home to you. Both of you. I mean that.

Pause. Windshield wipers. The baby cries again.

GRACE: I love...

Static.

JAMES: Grace?

GRACE: *(through static)*...love you...

JAMES: What?

GRACE: *(through static)* I said I love...

Her voice fades into the storm outside. The static completely overtakes Grace's transmission and the baby, then goes silent.

117

JAMES: Grace?

He fiddles with the CB.

JAMES: Goddamn it...

He rotates the knobs. The static escalates, then cuts off. Silence. Windshield wipers.

JAMES: Hello?

A croaky woman's voice comes through the CB.

CAROLYN: *(on radio)* James.

JAMES: That's very funny, Grace.

CAROLYN: Is that her name? You never told me her name.

Pause. Windshield wipers. Static.

JAMES: *(quietly)* Carolyn?

CAROLYN: I missed you.

Pause. Windshield wipers. Static.

JAMES: You sound different.

CAROLYN: Hard to sound like honey through a crushed larynx.

Pause. Windshield wipers. Static.

JAMES: I didn't mean for it to...You wouldn't stop screaming.

CAROLYN: If I had, you would've left.

Pause. Windshield wipers. Static.

JAMES: I'm sorry.

CAROLYN: For what.

JAMES: For everything.

CAROLYN: Everyone's always sorry for everything. No one wants to say what they actually did.

JAMES: I'm still sorry.

CAROLYN: Is that why you can't unload me from back here? The guilt?

JAMES: It's raining.

CAROLYN: Makes more sense to bury me in a storm. Less light. Less people.

JAMES: I'll get you out at the end of my shift. I promise.

CAROLYN: What a nice man.

Pause. Windshield wipers. Static.

CAROLYN: What do you talk about? You and her.

JAMES: We don't talk much. Never have.

CAROLYN: Not like us.

JAMES: I like the way her and I talk. The silences.

CAROLYN: I don't believe you.

JAMES: Sometimes we talk about the radio towers. Different things they remind us of.

CAROLYN: What do they look like now?

James looks out the window.

JAMES: Metal dinosaurs.

CAROLYN: Like the rallies?

JAMES: No. Real dinosaurs. But made of metal.

Pause. Windshield wipers. Static.

JAMES: What do you see?

CAROLYN: Nothing from back here, love.

Pause. Windshield wipers. Static.

CAROLYN: You remember the softball games?

James smiles.

JAMES: I do.

CAROLYN: Saturdays for the wives and Wednesdays for the girlfriends.

JAMES: Wednesdays.

CAROLYN: I liked them.

JAMES: Me, too.

He laughs to himself.

JAMES: One time Asa Butler tried to bring his wife on a Wednesday.

CAROLYN: He was the only one without a girlfriend.

JAMES: Sarge got so mad. Thought she would tell everyone.

CAROLYN: Did she?

JAMES: No. Asa was a good guy. He just didn't know how things worked.

CAROLYN: Are you a good guy, James?

Pause. Windshield wipers. Static.

JAMES: I could be.

CAROLYN: Maybe.

The trunk pops open on its own. James sits there, staring straight ahead.

JAMES: Please go away.

CAROLYN: I can't ever go away. You know that.

JAMES: You'll be underground soon.

CAROLYN: Wouldn't keep me from you. Neither would your wife. Or your little boy.

Pause. Windshield wipers. Static.

JAMES: Who told you about him?

CAROLYN: Heard him crying through the static.

Pause. Windshield wipers. Static. James closes his eyes.

CAROLYN: Well?

Pause. Windshield wipers. Static. A gospel song comes on the radio, crystal clear. James listens to it for a long time. He finally opens his eyes and speaks, almost to himself.

JAMES: I'm on my way.

He exits the car, the song still playing. Outside the car, James slowly walks to the trunk and stares into it. He doesn't move. The song continues to play.

Blackout.

End of play.

Valhalla Correctional

By Peter Ullian

Inspired by "We Take Care of Our Own" by Bruce Springsteen.

CHARACTERS

    JESS: mid-forties-ish. Married to Lev.

    LEV: mid-forties-ish. Married to Jess.

SETTING

    Jess and Lev's house.

TIME

    The Great Recession, or soon thereafter.

Lev and Jess. Mid-forties. Married for twenty years. They speak to us and to each other.

JESS: I'm Jess.

LEV: I'm Lev.

JESS: I'm an accountant. Or was.

LEV: I'm a novelist.

JESS: You're a novelist in the same way I'm a singer 'cause I sing "Cadillac Ranch" in the shower.

LEV: Fuck you.

JESS: Fuck you back.

LEV: *(to us)* I have two *published* novels. Well, one collection of linked short stories and one novel. Both published by respectable small presses.

JESS: Both out of print.

LEV: I still get short stories published.

JESS: Every two years. Maybe. You get paid in contributor's copies. You can't eat contributor's copies.

LEV: You loved that I was a writer when we met.

JESS: That's true. I did. Hunched over your laptop, coffee cup beside you, cigarette dangling from your mouth.

LEV: *(to us)* I don't smoke anymore.

JESS: And your hair.

LEV: I had great hair.

JESS: You still have great hair. That salt and pepper thing is really working for you. I love to tangle my fingers in those locks when we fuck.

LEV: Jess!

JESS: What?

LEV: *(indicating us)* Come on . . .

JESS: Oh.

(beat. to us)

I'm just kidding. We don't really fuck.

LEV: Jess!

JESS: What? *(to us)* We've been married twenty years, we have three kids, who has time to fuck?

LEV: *(to us)* We have normal marital relations, Ok?

JESS: Just not as often as we used to.

LEV: *(to us)* Well, we've got three kids.

JESS: Don't remind me. *(to us)* Anyway.

LEV: *(to us)* Anyway. Jess got laid off.

JESS: I got corporate downsized.

LEV: We saw it coming.

JESS: This was during the Great Recession. First they freeze salaries, stop giving cost of living raises, stop giving out bonuses—except for the executive level. 'Cause, y'know, they're special. They're the masters of the universe. My company hires a new upper executive guy, right in the middle of this economic disaster, and spends eighty thousand dollars redoing his office before he moves in. While the rest of us have a salary freeze. I didn't make eighty thousand dollars a year, and they spend that on his carpet and bookshelves. Then they make us take ten mandatory unpaid days off over the course of the summer—basically, one day a week. They send out this memo that under no circumstances are we to work on those unpaid days off. No e-mails, nothing.

LEV: Which is total bullshit.

JESS: Which is total bullshit, because if you don't work on those days, you'd be so behind on the four days you are working that you'd never be able to get caught up, or you'd stay at work until midnight every night, and you're not getting overtime, because you're salaried. So, I worked from home on those days.

LEV: You went in to work on one of them.

JESS: That's right. Unpaid leave day, and I end up going into work because otherwise there's no way to get the work done.

LEV: And they know this.

JESS: Oh, they know this all right. They think they own your labor. They don't really think you contract your labor to them for an agreed-upon wage. They own it. You're obligated to provide it whether they pay you for it or not. When the corporation's in trouble, it's all, "we're all in this together." But we're not all in this together. The guys at the top are only in it for themselves. They don't give a shit about you. They don't give a shit that your kid needs new shoes. They don't give a shit that you need to pay almost five hundred dollars a month for a Metro North pass to get to work whether you're working four or five days a week.

LEV: They don't give a shit about any of that.

JESS: They don't give a shit that you gave fifteen years to that company, your entire adult working life, almost. If you'd moved from company to company, you'd be making a shit load more money, but you stayed, because you foolishly thought loyalty counted for something.

LEV: Loyalty doesn't count for anything.

JESS: Loyalty counts for shit. The CEOs get their golden parachutes, the banks get their federal bailouts, the car companies get their government rescue, and the rest of us get three months severance and COBRA payments we can't possibly afford.

LEV: This was after Obamacare passed but before it was implemented.

JESS: And not only are there no jobs out there, but there's even fewer jobs if you're over forty.

LEV: We're both sending out resumes like crazy.

JESS: Bupkis.

LEV: Jackshit.

JESS: Nada. I mean, I get it. Forty something year-olds can't possibly be as good at crunching numbers as twenty-something year-olds, right? Because, you know, perky boobs over skill and experience any day, right? I'm sure those Barbie dolls can balance the books perfectly with those perky boobs.

LEV: I should have been doing the university teaching thing, starting as an adjunct, working my way up the ladder. By the time Jess lost her corporate job, all my writer friends had university jobs, and I had a ten year hole in my resume.

JESS: For ten years, Lev was the stay-at-home parent. Taking the kids to the library, dropping them off and picking them up from school, taking them to ballet and karate and violin lessons, cooking dinner, changing diapers, doing laundry. Writing his novels during naptime. In other words, Lev didn't work.

LEV: Fuck you, I did too work. Raising kids is as hard as the work you did, even if you don't get paid for it. But by the time I'm back on the job market, something like seventy five percent of university professors are adjuncts with almost no chance of making assistant professor anymore, ever. Higher education had changed. So, we start to adjust expectations.

JESS: Lev thinks he's going to be a prison guard.

LEV: Our neighbor across the street was sixty when he became a prison guard. There's no age limit as long as you can pass the test and the physical. It's got good benefits.

JESS: Our neighbors across the street are Republicans. We didn't know from Republicans until we moved out of the city. Apparently, they're not just on Fox News. They're your friends and neighbors.

LEV: We never imagined.

JESS: I was making a joke about Republicans and they said "we're Republicans."

LEV: And she laughed.

JESS: And I laughed. I thought they were joking.

LEV: They weren't joking.

JESS: They're actual Republicans.

LEV: And they're nice.

JESS: They're super-nice. They are the nicest sweetest most neighborly neighbors you could ask for.

LEV: They feed our cats when we're out of town.

JESS: They give our diabetic cat his insulin shots when we're out of town!

LEV: They watched our kids when they were small.

JESS: I was afraid our kids were gonna end up reading Ayn Rand pop-up books or something.

LEV: They still pick up our kids from school when we're in a jam.

JESS: You make a lot of surprising friends when you're a grown-up, I guess.

LEV: So, I figured, a sixty year old guy can be a correctional officer, why can't I? I thought it would provide some good material. I figured I could write a novel about it on my days off.

JESS: Another novel you can't get published. How many unpublished novels have you got on your laptop?

LEV: My agent says the industry has changed.

JESS: *(to us)* He still has an agent. He's a charity case.

LEV: Fuck you. There's no such thing as a mid-list anymore.

JESS: You were never mid-list. You were at the bottom of the list.

LEV: Fuck you twice. *(to us)* Self-publishing isn't really an option. The stories you hear about wild self-publishing success are flukes. Most self-published authors can count their annual sales on one hand.

JESS: So, you failed as a novelist, and you decided you'd be a prison guard?

LEV: I didn't fail as a novelist, I'm a published novelist. But I figured, publishers love fiction if the author is writing about something they actually did—it creates a narrative they can sell. You know, "prison guard writes prison guard novel." Doesn't even matter if the writing is shit. And my writing isn't shit. So, I thought, if I did something interesting, and wrote about it, that might be something that could sell. I'm too old to be a cop or join the military. But not to be a prison guard.

JESS: You're not a tough guy, Lev. Writing stories about tough guys does not make you a tough guy.

LEV: I've taken care of three kids for ten years. I'm as tough as they come, babe.

JESS: Right.

LEV: Anyway, I aced the prison guard written test. And the background check. So, then comes the physical. I run around an obstacle course, drag a dummy, lift stuff, and all the time, I've got Springsteen's song "Dead Man Walking" going through my head. I mean, what if one day I have to escort a guy to the chair?

JESS: New York State doesn't have the death penalty and Westchester County Prison doesn't have a death row!

LEV: It's in Valhalla, New York. Isn't that just so, I don't know, poetic? A prison in Valhalla. I mean, talk about great material. Maybe I could write a fantasy novel about a prison in Westchester County and all the guards are Nordic deities who need the work, because no one worships them anymore, so they had to convert Valhalla into a county prison and rent themselves out as correctional officers. *American Gods* meets *Percy Jackson* meets *The Shawshank Redemption*. Blockbuster potential. Hollywood high concept. I could write the shit out of that.

JESS: You could, actually.

LEV: Thank you.

JESS: You're a really good writer.

LEV: I know. But thank you for saying it.

JESS: Tell them about the physical, for God's sake.

LEV: Ok. So, I'm doing all this running and shit, you have to open a jail door, turn the key to lock it again, run up stairs, run down stairs, I'm huffing and I'm puffing, but I'm as fast—

JESS: Not as fast.

LEV: Fast enough. And as strong as people half my age.

JESS: Changing diapers really builds that upper body strength.

LEV: Carrying around your off-spring day after day for ten years does. Look at these biceps.

(He shows off his biceps.)

JESS: You do have nice biceps.

LEV: Thank you.

JESS: Sometimes I like to brace my arms against them when we fuck.

LEV: Jess!

JESS: What? Oh, right. *(to us)* I'm just kidding, we're married, we don't fuck.

LEV: Will you cut it out?

JESS: Too bad you don't have abdominal muscles like your biceps. All you had to do was twenty sit-ups in one minute.

LEV: I did nineteen.

JESS: Nineteen! You couldn't do one more sit-up? What's wrong with you?

LEV: I was afraid I was going to fart!

(Beat. Jess has never heard this detail before.)

JESS: What?

LEV: When we got there, they said, some of you will pass gas when you do the sit-up test. And the guy holding down my legs had a surgical mask on just in case.

JESS: Oh my God.

LEV: I didn't want to be the prison guard who farted! I knew I'd already be the nerdy writer-guy college-boy prison guard. The rest of my colleagues were very blue collar guys. Totally guys from a Bruce Springsteen song.

JESS: *(to us)* He drives around with the windows down on our 2002 Honda Odyssey minivan blasting "Thunder Road."

LEV: Springsteen's written albums full of songs about these guys, and I love those songs, but those songs aren't about me.

JESS: "Growing Up" is about you. Because you need to do that. "Queen of The Supermarket" is about you. Because you buy the groceries.

LEV: Why do you try to emasculate me because I raised our kids for ten years?

JESS: "Fifty Seven Channels and Nothing On" is about how you hog the remote, I think. "Your Own Worst Enemy" is definitely about you because that's what you are and "Dream Baby Dream" is also about you because that's all you do. "Hungry Heart" is about your ability to eat an entire pepperoni pizza by yourself in one sitting.

LEV: Are you finished?

JESS: "From Small Things (Big Things One Day Come)" is probably about your penis.

LEV: OhMyGod! What is wrong with you?

JESS: You mean to tell me we're on public assistance now because you were afraid you were going to fart?

LEV: I just paused for a second to get control of everything going on gastrointestinally and then all of a sudden time was up.

JESS: Oh my God. We cashed out our retirement savings, the kids qualify for free meals at school, we cancelled the cable TV, the minivan bumper is attached with duct tape because we can't afford to take it to the shop, we can't eat out or take the kids to the movies, we had to cancel all the kids after-school activities, we have to get HEAP assistance to heat our home in the winter, we can't pay our synagogue membership dues, the mortgage is in forbearance, I have to buy groceries with an EBT card, do you know how the people in line look at me? They scowl at me. They do. They look down on me. All because you can't control your farts?

LEV: I didn't want to be the farting intellectual college-boy prison guard who failed at writing novels for the rest of my working life!

JESS: You know what Cody asked me yesterday? "Are we poor?" That's what your son asked me.

(Beat.)

LEV: What did you tell him?

JESS: I said, yes, we are.

(Beat.)

I didn't tell him we're poor because Daddy can't do twenty sit-ups in a minute's time without farting.

LEV: I totally can!

(He gets on the floor and starts doing sit-ups.)

JESS: Cut it out.

LEV: One.

JESS: Stop.

LEV: You stop. Two.

JESS: Oh my God.

LEV: Three.

JESS: You don't have to prove anything to me.

LEV: Four.

JESS: I don't care if you can do twenty sit-ups in a minute.

LEV: Five.

JESS: That's not why I married you.

LEV: Why did you marry me? Six.

JESS: I married you for your pretty lips and your thick head of hair and because you fuck with diligence and enthusiasm and can go down on me like nobody's business.

LEV: Jess!

JESS: What?

LEV: Seven. Ow.

JESS: You Ok?

LEV: I think I pulled something.

JESS: Oh, great.

LEV: Help me up.

(She helps him up.)

JESS: Where's it hurt?

LEV: My groin.

JESS: You pulled your groin doing six sit-ups.

LEV: Seven. I twisted my body funny.

JESS: You're pathetic.

LEV: *(lashing out)* You are! You didn't even send out a resume until your severance was exhausted!

JESS: *(fighting back)* Because it was your turn to work!

LEV: You think raising Irish triplets isn't work?

JESS: We're not Irish and I've been working since I was sixteen when my father bailed and never paid a dime in child support or alimony! I made your career possible! After grad school, you wouldn't have been able to write that novel with a five hundred dollar advance if I wasn't working! You think I wanted to have a career as an accountant? I had dreams too, you know! I wanted to be an actress!

LEV: You were a good actress.

JESS: I know!

LEV: I never told you to give it up!

JESS: No, you just decided to write a novel full-time on a five hundred dollar advance! How did you think we were we going to pay the bills?

LEV: People work survival jobs and still pursue their acting careers, you know!

JESS: Not when they're supporting a full-time novelist with not even part-time earnings!

LEV: I supported you too, you know! When we were students I paid all the bills!

JESS: Because you had that fancy-schmancy scholarship and I was working my way through school and living on tips!

LEV: This isn't about us! It's about our kids! I've been sending out resumes since they froze your salary. I've been trying. I got nothing. It's not a question of whose turn it is. It's a question of who can get a job to feed our kids!

JESS: Do you know what it's like? Do you know how emotionally debilitating it is to give fifteen years to a place and then be dumped? You know how that makes a person feel? What it does to a person's confidence? To her self-esteem? To be treated like you're a piece of shit stuck to the bottom of someone's twenty-five hundred dollar Gucci crocodile horsebit loafers? That's half my annual bonus in a good year when they were still giving bonuses to accountants, and some asshole puts that on his feet and uses it to step in dogshit?

(Beat.)

LEV: I'm sorry what they did to you. I'm sorry I failed the sit-up test.

JESS: I don't want to talk about it. Tell them about the Bat Mitzvah.

LEV: Ok.

(Beat.)

135

So, in the middle of this, our daughter, Leah, she's coming up on her Bat Mitzvah.

JESS: And we have no idea how we're going to pay for anything.

LEV: And she's got to officially convert.

JESS: Because I'm not "technically" Jewish in the whole matrilineal sense.

LEV: And the mikva and whatnot costs money.

JESS: And the reception?

LEV: Leah's friends are all having these awesome expensive parties.

JESS: With DJs.

LEV: And caterers.

JESS: In ballrooms.

LEV: With bands.

JESS: And swag.

LEV: And hors-d'oeuvre.

JESS: Like these little lamb-chops on a stick.

LEV: And canapes.

JESS: And a taco bar.

LEV: And mini-quiches.

JESS: And a chocolate fountain. And we can't afford that. We can't afford a chocolate fountain!

LEV: So, basically, we're fucked.

> *(Beat.)*

JESS: And then something amazing happens.

LEV: The synagogue pays for the mikva.

JESS: And the local theatre?

LEV: Leah is really into theatre.

JESS: She was in their production of *To Kill a Mockingbird.*

LEV: As Scout.

JESS: She was amazing. She takes after me, of course.

LEV: And she takes dance classes there.

JESS: Which she pays for herself with the money she earns babysitting.

LEV: Because we can't afford to pay for her lessons anymore.

(Beat. He is emotional)

She's an amazing kid. I'm so, so freaking proud of her.

(Beat.)

JESS: So, the theatre . . .

LEV: The theatre offers their space to us for the reception.

JESS: For free.

LEV: Because they love our daughter.

JESS: Almost as much as we do.

LEV: And our cantor from the synagogue –

JESS: Tovah –

LEV: She organizes a team of people to make food.

JESS: And our neighbors from across the street.

LEV: The Republicans.

JESS: They bake a cake.

LEV: The most beautiful cake.

JESS: They're not even Jewish.

LEV: It's the best cake ever.

JESS: And they help decorate the theatre with streamers and shit. And Leah's friends —

(Beat. She is emotional)

They make a playlist on an iPod of all the songs the kids are listening to these days.

LEV: And we play it over the theatre's sound system.

JESS: And the kids dance like crazy.

LEV: And it's this amazing blend of people. Because that's the kind of town we live in. And those are the kind of friends Leah has. I mean, one week she's at a friend's Bat Mitzvah, the next she's at a Quinceañera. We live on Sesame Street. We even have muppets.

JESS: Lev does a Hanukkah puppet show every year.

LEV: Jews, gentiles, black, white, Asian, Hispanic. All dancing to Bruno Mars and the Cha-Cha Slide and the Hora!

JESS: We teach everyone to dance the Hora!

LEV: And we lift Leah up on the chair!

JESS: And the food!

LEV: Trays of baked ziti and broccoli rabe and quiche and these amazing salads with homemade dressing and bowls of egg salad and baskets of bagels from the kosher place in Rockland county. And guess who picked up and paid for those?

JESS: Our neighbors. The Republicans. And they also ordered a shitload of pizza.

LEV: No meat, it's not exactly kosher, but no meat and dairy, and no *trayf*.

JESS: And the kids, all sweaty from dancing, devour the pizza like it's manna from heaven. Which it sort of is.

LEV: And it's the best party ever.

JESS: It's not fancy but it's funky and quirky and down-to-earth and it's perfect for Leah and her arty multi-culti friends.

LEV: And afterwards a dozen people stay and help us cleanup for I don't know how many hours.

JESS: Our friends and neighbors really came through for us. Our entire community. The shul, the neighborhood, family, friends, everyone. Jews, gentiles, old and young. They took care of us.

LEV: And we have all these left-overs!

JESS: We won't have to feed our kids Ramen for a month.

(Beat. JESS produces two bowls of ziti, and they eat in silence. It's really good.)

JESS: You know, you can still write that novel. About the prison in Valhalla.

LEV: I don't know anything about prisons.

JESS: Stephen Crane didn't know anything about the Civil War when he wrote *The Red Badge of Courage.* You should totally write your Valhalla Prison novel. Who knows? Maybe this time things will work out. Maybe you'll have a best-seller.

LEV: And if I don't?

JESS: Don't be so negative. You could totally write the shit out of that thing.

(Beat.)

LEV: You know what? I totally could.

(Beat.)

What should I call it? The novel.

(Beat. Jess thinks.)

JESS: *Valhalla Correctional.*

(Beat.)

LEV: That's a great fucking title.

JESS: I know, right?

(Beat. They eat.)

LEV: This baked ziti is so good.

JESS: You know why, right?

LEV: Tell me.

JESS: Because it's made with love.

They eat in silence.

End of play.

Pick Up Beds

By K. Frithjof Peterson

Inspired by "When You're Alone" by Bruce Springsteen

.

CHARACTERS

> JIM: 20s. In love.

> MARK: 20s. Not in love.

SETTING

> Outside a bar. The bumper, tailgate and bed of a Chevy Pickup.

TIME

> When things should change.

MARK exits the bar and sits on the bumper of a Chevy pickup truck. There's probably an American flag somewhere on the truck. JIM is slower getting there.

JIM: *(to MARK)* Their bathrooms were disgusting. The whole bar smelled. *(to the bar)* Your bar smells!

MARK: Just sit.

JIM: It had an odor.

MARK: Sit.

JIM: *(to the bar)* Your entire bar smells! Nasty and funky! We were leaving anyway!

MARK: You done?

JIM: And if you play a song with "revolution" in the lyrics you have to assume the furniture will get danced on. The furniture will get danced on!

MARK stands on the bumper - bouncing the truck a little. Maybe a seductive dance. He sings a bit to Jim. Something they heard in the bar. Something hopeful, featuring the word "revolution." Something like "Revolution" by the Beatles.

MARK displays a carved up, stuffed animal.

JIM: That's dark. Maybe we don't sit right here? Someone gutted that. Like on purpose.

MARK: Just sit with me.

MARK hands him the stuffed animal.

JIM: Oh my god, it smells like piss. Why does everything smell horrible?

JIM throws it back in the bed.

MARK: Please, sit with me.

JIM: I don't wanna sit. I wanna break something.

MARK fishes around the bed. He finds a wire coat hanger. He gives it to JIM. JIM tries unsuccessfully to "break" the hanger.

MARK: Better?

JIM: Meh...

> *JIM tosses it back into the bed. MARK finds a hollow picture frame and displays it to frame his face.*

MARK: Are you ready to sit now?

> *JIM sits.*

MARK: I don't love you anymore.

> *JIM takes the picture frame from MARK and returns it to the bed of the truck.*

MARK: I mean I'm not in love with you.

JIM: ...

MARK: ...

JIM: ...

MARK: Who's trash do you think this is? Truck owner's? Random passersby?

JIM: Is this cuz I threw a shot glass at the bartender?

MARK: No.

JIM: Cuz that was for you. I defended your dancing.

MARK: Thanks for defending my honor.

> *MARK pulls a lei out of the bed. He tries to lei JIM.*

JIM: Gross.

MARK: It happened at dinner.

JIM: What did I do at dinner?

MARK: Nothing.

JIM: *(it doesn't make sense)* Well that makes sense. How long has this been going on?

MARK: It happened at dinner.

JIM: Is there someone else?

MARK: No. It happened at dinner. I don't know what else to tell you.

JIM: Tell me how it feels to not love me anymore.

MARK: Not great.

JIM: Nifty.

MARK: It feels like I just had to say something honest and horrible. It feels like I'm telling someone who really enjoys singing along with the radio that they can't sing.

JIM: Fuck you. Do not go there. I'm a fantastic singer.

MARK: I know.

JIM: This is silly. I'm not even sure why I'm entertaining it. There's a natural progression to things. Things naturally progress.

MARK: I don't think so. Not -

JIM: This is not a natural progression. First we fall out of love. It's a process. Then we resent each other.

MARK: I don't resent you.

JIM: Exactly. So I refuse to accept this.

MARK: Well, it happened. I wish it didn't. Life would be easier if it didn't. But it did.

JIM: Doesn't sound like much of anything actually happened.

MARK: ...

JIM: Cuz you're saying it just... Poof - gone.

MARK: Yeah.

JIM: Without anything specific you can point to.

MARK: Yeah.

JIM: See that's... That's not how things work. Things don't just vanish. Things change. Slowly. They don't - poof!

MARK finds a book in the pickup bed. It's rain soaked.

MARK: There's a lot of books back here. I think I'm gonna keep this one.

JIM takes the book and throws it back.

JIM: You don't get a souvenir.

MARK: I don't think things change slowly.

JIM: Well, they do. So if it suddenly wasn't there at dinner, maybe it never was.

MARK: Not true.

JIM: Makes more sense than "poof!"

MARK: Every time you painted my nails - in love. Every time I forgot to clean the lint trap and you marched it up the stairs to show me - in love. Every time you smelled the wet coffee grounds before you threw them out - in love.

JIM: Let's go home. You do a load of laundry. I make some coffee. We paint your nails.

MARK: So you paint my nails and it doesn't work and then that's - what? We break something beautiful to prove it wasn't beautiful? Great. I'd rather save us that.

JIM: Maybe you should have to go through that - for my sake. For my sake, maybe I need to see it fail and break and get to be angry with you instead of just shocked and confused.

MARK: Is that what you really want?

JIM: Yes.

MARK: That's sad.

JIM: We need a transitional period. Or hey, here's a thought, maybe we actually work on whatever's wrong with us and -

MARK: I disagree.

JIM: That we deserve a chance?

MARK: I don't think we progressively heal. I don't think things get progressively sadder. I think things break and there's no going back. And I believe something can happen and in an instant we can heal. I have to believe that. Because life doesn't feel long enough to heal anymore. It really doesn't.

JIM: That sounds lazy. Lacks any accountability. And makes me not respect you.

MARK hops in the back of the pickup and tosses the gutted stuffed animal onto the sidewalk.

MARK: What did that change? You think people are gonna stop throwing things in here now?

MARK pulls something else out and tosses it on the sidewalk.

MARK: How about now? You think the owner is gonna say, "Well, looks like someone got this started, I should probably go ahead and clean this out now." How long do you think most of this stuff has been in here? That's not how things change. Here.

MARK starts dumping arm fulls of random things out of the pickup. He empties the bed. There's a pile of weird stuff at JIM's feet.

MARK: Now there's a chance.

JIM: Where you gonna stay?

MARK: Probably with Ali.

JIM: I figured. You getting an Uber?

MARK: I don't know. Sure. Maybe I'll walk.

JIM: Cuz I don't wanna walk home alone. Whatever we are now, I still don't wanna walk home alone. Don't do that to me.

MARK: Ok.

They just stand there.

JIM: I'm not leading. I didn't start this.

MARK holds out his hand.

JIM: No. That's... No. Just walk.

MARK starts to walk.

JIM: But sort of close to me.

MARK waits for him. They sort of walk off together.

End of play.

Birthday Wishes

by Nikkole Salter

Inspired by "Secret Garden" by Bruce Springsteen

CHARACTERS

> MOM: 60+ African American woman with Alzheimer's, completely unaware of (or in denial about) just how bad her condition has become.

> SON: 29 to 35-year old African American man in deep need for truth

SETTING

> 2010ish, American urbana

Nursing home suite. Late. Remnants of a small birth-day linger in the room - cheap

bouquet, cut cake, etc. Mom sits in her night clothes watching Jerry Springer or some

such smut. The son knocks. The mother looks around and dismisses the sound as

another sign that she is indeed going crazy. There's another knock.

SON: Mom?

MOM: Roy?

SON: It's me.

MOM: Boy.

SON: Can I come in?

The mom opens the door. Son embraces mom.

MOM: What you doin' here?

SON: It's your birthday ain't it?

MOM: My birthday was yesterday.

SON: *(gingerly)* No. Mom. October sixteenth? Your birthday is -

MOM: I know my own birthday, dummy. What I mean is that it's after midnight. My birthday was yesterday.

SON: Oh.

MOM: You late.

SON: *(realizing)* Oh, okay. Okay. For a minute there I thought -

MOM: Thought what?

SON: You were having another…*(a gesture signifying, "episode")*

MOM: What's *(mimicking the gesture)*?

SON: A… a moment.

MOM: I don't have moments.

SON: You do.

MOM: Your brain don't immediately begin to shrivel up at diagnosis, you know.

SON: I didn't mean -

MOM: Y'all 'bout to drive me crazy with that. You should've seen Sharon and them earlier.

Takin' the cake knife from me like I'm seven years old. Like I can't cut my own cake. The cake I baked!

SON: Wait: I gave Sharon money to buy you a cake. I gave her forty dollars -

MOM: Since when we eat that nasty supermarket machine-made cake?

SON: I told her to get it from a bakery.

MOM: When have I ever served y'all a slice of that? Every birthday this family has I always make my lemon cake with lemon glaze-

SON: If you give us the recipe, we could make it for you and we wouldn't have to buy -

MOM: Y'all can't cook.

SON: I can cook.

MOM: Y'all can't even do grilled cheese without supervision.

SON: Say who?

MOM: Say me.

SON: You got us confused, ma. Unlike Sharon, I can follow directions. If I knew the ingredients -

MOM: Don't you start with that again. You know I don't tell nobody 'bout my cake.

SON: We yo' people, ma. You gon' take it to the grave and let it die?

MOM: I'ma tell the grands. If you'd get married and have some kids maybe -

SON: What you think we gon' do? Sell it to Duncan Hines?

MOM: You not gon' do nothin' 'cause I'm not gon' give it to you.

SON: Mom -

MOM: 'Sides, it's not just the ingredients. It's the technique of how you put it all together. You can have all the ingredients you want, but if you ain't got the technique, if you ain't got no elbow grease, it won't matter.

SON: If you tell us how, if we had the ingredients -

MOM: It don't matter what's in it. All that matter is you like it, right? It work for you. It fill you up. It put a smile on your face. It's good, ain't it?

SON: Yes.

MOM: It don't matter how. It only matter that. That's all that matter.

SON:

A few moments pass.

MOM: I said that to Sharon too. She had the nerve - trying to get on me for baking. Like I'm a child.

SON: Doctor said you should be taking it easy.

MOM: It don't take me but twenty-minutes to whip up no cake batter. Hell, fifteen. I been doin' it since I was 9 years old. I could do it with my eyes closed.

SON: Things is different now.

MOM: Y'all need to stop it with the doom and gloom. Y'all so dramatic. Ain't nothin' even change yet. Sharon got the kids walkin' 'roun here askin' me, "Nana, what's our name?" Like I'm just learnin' ABC's. Twins talkin' down to me, talkin' 'bout "Nana, what's our name?" I said, "Stupid one and stupid two."

SON: That's cold ma.

MOM: That's what y'all get, acting all willy-nilly. Payin' the nurse all that money to spend the night. Ridiculous.

Moments pass.

SON: So, y'all had fun.

MOM: We did. Where were you?

SON: I…I over slept.

MOM: Humph.

SON: You make me a plate?

MOM: 'scuse me?

SON: You let them eat all the - You knew I was comin'!

MOM: I ain't knowed no such thing. You ain't called nobody. Damn near over a week.

SON: I needed some time. *(beat)* I wasn't gon' miss your birthday.

MOM:

SON: Hell, it could be the last birthday you remember.

MOM: I'm gon' kick you. The last birthday I remember. I got the memory of an elephant. No matter what happens, you best believe I don't never forget.

SON: Alright, ma.

He laughs. She hands him the plate. He eats a few bites.

MOM: So, you laughin'. You feel better now?

SON: I do. *(beat)* I mean, I still got questions.

MOM: Questions.

SON: Yeah. I think I'm entitled to -

MOM: Oh, no. See - I'm not doin' this with you tonight, son.

SON: Ma -

MOM: It's my birthday. What kind of thing is this to do on your mama's birthday -

SON: You just said it wasn't your birthday.

MOM: I know what I said -

SON: That's why I waited. I knew you'd say that. But it ain't your birthday. Your birthday was yesterday. Ain't no stores open, you ain't got to run no where. Ain't no phone calls you got to make, 'cause everybody sleep. You ain't got company, and expecting any either. It ain't the Lord's time with you. And you wide awake, feelin' fine. Ain't no reason why you can't talk to me.

MOM: So you cornerin' me?

SON: I am. 'Cause when I ask you regular, you dodge. Or you make like I'm being disrespectful.

MOM: You is.

SON: How?

MOM: What son question his mama about her -

SON: See, I'm not asking you about your - I'm not questioning you. // We both grown now, mama. I understand how things go. I understand what happen in life. I just -

MOM: It ain't proper. You ain't as grown as me. I'm still your mother. I don't care what you understand.

SON: I ain't got no judgement. I just want to know. I got a right to know, don't I?

MOM: Know what?

SON: Mom -

MOM: You mean to tell me you don't know. Did you have socks and underwear? // Did you have schoolin' and food and a place to rest your head. Did you have love and support and family-

SON: It's not about that. I'm not saying that I didn't have. That's not the point, ma. Don't I get to know? What if something happens to me?

MOM: What's going to happen to you?

SON: When the doctor asks me if I have a family history of prostate cancer, what do I say? I don't know?

MOM: Tell them no. You don't.

SON: What if I have siblings? // Nieces and nephews?

MOM: What you mean, what if you got siblings? Sharon ain't yo' sister now?

SON: Other siblings. Other half siblings. Doesn't a man have a right to know who his siblings are. What if I hit on my sister at the club?

MOM: You shouldn't be in the club.

SON: Or wherever. The club ain't the only place I - in church.

MOM: You hit on women in the Lord's house?

SON: Doesn't a man have a right to know who his people are?

MOM: You don't know who your people are?

SON: I don't mean -

MOM: You don't know who took care of you?

SON: You know what I'm talking about.

MOM: I don't know why you want to rip this family apart. Desecrate your father's memory.

SON: Did daddy know?

MOM: *(beat)* Is you tryin' to get my pressure up?

SON: Mom -

MOM: Hush! Now I gotta - move!

Mom pulls out a blood pressure machine, and begins to open the cuff and place it on her arm.

SON: Mom. Don't take your pressure.

MOM: I can feel it going up.

SON: Mom.

Son places his hands on the cuff.

SON: Please. Please. Please. Please. Please, mama. You not gonna be here forever. Please, before you... before you forget.

Moments pass.

MOM: What do you want to know, son?

SON: *(beat)* Did he hurt you? I mean, was I conceived out of some kind of trauma.

MOM: No.

SON: Did daddy know?

MOM: He loved you as his own.

SON: But did he know?

MOM: What you want from me Roy? Huh? What?

SON: *(beat)* What was he like?

MOM: He was nice.

SON: Do I look like him?

MOM:

SON: Sharon used to say that I was adopted 'cause I ain't look like nobody in this family.

MOM: She said that to you? I'll kill her.

SON: She would say y'all found me on the street.

MOM: Ain't nobody found you. I gave birth to you.

SON: But I always wondered why I didn't look like daddy. (beat) Is it 'cause I look like him?

Mom looks to her son.

MOM: (beat) Y'all favor. You do. Y'all...

Mom starts to cry. Son comforts her.

SON: Mama don't cry. Don't - I'm not trying to make you sad, ma. I don't have no judgement. None. I just.... I'm going to have children one day. I want to be able to tell them the truth. I want to be able to tell them everything. I just want to know what happened. I want to know who he is. Who I am. That's all. That's all, I promise. I'm not mad with you. I love you. I love daddy. I just...I just want to know. That's all. That's all.

He wipes her tears.

MOM: Okay.

She rises and goes to a secret place and pulls out an old box. She offers the box to her son with a smile.

MOM: That's all I got.

SON: How long you had this?

MOM: I been tendin' to it since you been here.

He looks to her in amazement, and she goads him forward. He opens it and pulls out an old photo and a handkerchief. He looks at the photo for a long time.

SON: This my daddy?

MOM:

SON: Did you love him, mama?

MOM: I did.

SON: What was he like then?

MOM: He thought he was so smooth. He was country.

SON: What's his name?

MOM: Why you want to know his name for?

SON: So I can go see him. Look him up. Meet him before -

MOM: Bobby?

SON: Huh?

MOM: Robert Franklin Fairweather.

SON: No, it's Roy. Your son. Uncle Bobby ain't -

MOM: Bobby, what you doin' in my things? You rascal. Gimme my - !

She snatches the box and the photo.

SON: Mom? Quit playin', now. That ain't fair -

MOM: I'ma tell mama you don't put it down right now. I'm gonna scream.

He looks to her. She starts to scream. He hands her the

box. She stops and composes herself.

MOM: I'ma tell mama.

SON: *(very long beat)* Don't tell mama. I promise I'll never look through your things again.

MOM: You better not.

SON: I promise.

MOM: What you swear on?

SON: I put that on my mama cake.

MOM: Mama made some cake?!

SON: Yep. And I'll give you some if you don't tell on me.

He offers her the plate. She considers, then takes it and eats.

MOM: This my favorite.

SON: Mine too.

MOM: You know what mama put in it to make it so moist?

SON: I don't. It's a secret.

MOM: I'ma find out.

She eats. He breaks down in tears.

End of play.

Growin' Up, Or I Was a Teenage Bruce Springsteen!

By Steve Feffer

Inspired by "Growin' Up" by Bruce Springsteen

CHARACTERS

THE COSMIC KID: in full costume dress.

THE JUKEBOX GRADUATE: a first mate.

FATHER RAY: according to Bruce, has seen *The Bells of St. Mary* too many times and also, again according to Bruce, perhaps trying to do his best Pat O'Brien, "Hollywood's Irishman-in-residence."

THE KID'S MOTHER.

BOBBY SOXER ELVIS: the 1960s Elvis that came out of the army, the Hollywood Elvis.

ELVIS, the 1950s Elvis, as we prefer to remember him. Played by the same actor as BOBBY.

TIME AND PLACE

A Catholic School, including Father Ray's office and the school's gym. Day and then midnight. The early 1960s.

At rise: Father Ray's office. THE COSMIC KID sits sulking in a chair. THE KID'S MOTHER is there distressed and is engaged animatedly with FATHER RAY.

MOTHER: He did what?

FATHER RAY: He… urinated in his desk.

MOTHER: Urinated?

FATHER RAY: Made pee pee...

MOTHER: I know what urinating is. But in his desk?

FATHER RAY: Yes.

MOTHER: I'm sorry, I'm just having a hard time understanding this.

> *(To THE COSMIC KID)*

I mean, they let you go to the bathroom at this school right?

THE COSMIC KID: Oh, yeah, they let us go. A few times a day…

MOTHER: *(While hitting his pompadour hair with her purse)* So why didn't you go?

THE COSMIC KID: I did. In my desk.

MOTHER: Why wouldn't you go to the?…

FATHER RAY: The potties?…

THE COSMIC KID: The potties?

MOTHER: *(Hitting him again in the head with her purse)* The Toilets! Whatever they have that isn't your desk?

THE COSMIC KID: I don't know! It just seemed like the right thing to do at the time. All these kids, at school, just talking about this homecoming thing. You know, this dance. And the football game. And it just made me feel like I needed to piss.

MOTHER: In your desk?

THE COSMIC KID: Yeah.

MOTHER: *(Hits him in the head again with her purse.)* Is there something wrong with you?

THE COSMIC KID: I don't think so.

MOTHER: I mean, is there something in your mind, that maybe isn't making sense of things.

THE COSMIC KID: Like if I'd been hit in the head repeatedly with a purse.

MOTHER hits him again in the head with her purse.

FATHER RAY: Excuse me: Can I be frank here?

THE COSMIC KID: Like Father Frank, right? From *The Bells of St. Mary.* You've seen that, right?

FATHER RAY: Yes, I've seen it. We've all seen it.

MOTHER: Father, tell him. Tell him that peeing in one's desk at school is madness. It's sick. It's demented. It's not Catholic.

FATHER RAY: We try not to judge in that way, as that is certainly not the Lord's way...

MOTHER: But Father, Father Frank...

FATHER RAY: Ray...

MOTHER: Ray. Frank. Whatever. Surely our Lord would have something to say about peeing in a Catholic school desk.

FATHER RAY: I don't believe that's in the scriptures.

MOTHER: Ask him why. Please. He won't tell us. All he does is sit in his room, all day long, and...

FATHER RAY: Now, well, the Lord does have something to say about *that*.

MOTHER: ... His guitar. Play his guitar.

FATHER RAY: Oh, well, a little quiet music can be just what is needed to calm such a turbulent soul... While I prefer Bing, I even let my hair down to a little Sinatra now and then...

MOTHER: It's not quiet music. It's not quiet at all...

FATHER RAY: *(Gasp)* Not... Pat Boone?

MOTHER: Worse. Much worse. Ask him, Father.

FATHER RAY: Son, why would a nice boy, from a good family, that seems to get good marks in school...

MOTHER: *(Whispering)* His marks are terrible, Father...

FATHER RAY: Well, who... *(beat) goes* to school. Why would that boy make pee pee in his desk?

THE COSMIC KID: Well, there is one thing.

FATHER RAY: Yes...

MOTHER: Yes...

THE COSMIC KID: The other night...

FATHER RAY: Yes, go on.

THE COSMIC KID: It was midnight. And I was out walking. And, well, I think...

FATHER: Yes...

THE COSMIC KID: I got bit by somethin'.

FATHER RAY: Bit...

MOTHER: Oh, my God...

FATHER RAY: Was it a dog?

THE COSMIC KID: Worse, Father.

FATHER RAY: Worse... Was it?... Oh, no...

MOTHER: What, Father...

FATHER RAY: Was it... Him?!!!

THE COSMIC KID: Who?

FATHER RAY: Him. Him. The devil himself?

THE COSMIC KID: Worse, Father.

FATHER RAY: Worse than the devil himself?

MOTHER: Worse than the Devil?...

> *MOTHER faints.*

FATHER RAY: Please, son, tell us. At last we might be getting somewhere...

THE COSMIC KID: Shouldn't we get her some water or something...

FATHER RAY: Happens all time... Just keep going...

THE COSMIC KID: It wasn't a dog and it wasn't the devil. For you see, Father:

FATHER RAY: *(Breathless)* Yes...

THE COSMIC KID: The moon was full. Hair was growing out of my face, hands and palms.

FATHER RAY: I knew it had something to do with *that*...All that time by yourself...

THE COSMIC KID: My teeth and nails grew and a guitar fell around my neck. I looked into a light. And then: I was a teenage werewolf!

FATHER RAY grabs THE COSMIC KID. And with a well-rehearsed move, swings him around and ties him to a chair, as if this is clearly not the first time he has done this to a student. He takes out a large silver cross attached to a string. MOTHER wakes in that moment.

MOTHER: Father, is this some kind of new form of confession?

FATHER RAY: In a way.

MOTHER: What are you doing to him?

FATHER RAY: Hypno-therapy. You see, your son was bitten by a wolf. While this alone may not have any negative effect on him—other than the obvious negative effects of being bitten by a wolf—this biting coupled with his predisposition toward the devil's music, has turned him into a...werewolf...

MOTHER: A werewolf?

FATHER RAY: Now, once I complete the hypno-therapy, he will become a normal boy like those others in his school. He will become the lawyer your husband wanted, or an author that you wanted. He will even like girls again...

MOTHER: He doesn't like girls?...

FATHER RAY: I was just assuming.

MOTHER: Does this work?

FATHER RAY: Oh, yes, I've done it many times to many of our students.

(Beat.)

For example, look at that boy over there.

Lights up on a young ELVIS PRESLEY from the 1950s. However, rather than the sneering leather-clad Elvis that we cherish, this ELVIS [BOBBY SOXER ELVIS] is neatly pressed into a high school letter sweater, saddle shoes and slacks, along with neatly combed hair.

FATHER RAY (cont'd): He used to look like this.

A picture of Elvis from 1956 appears—maybe even the "Elvis Presley" [1956] LP cover.

THE COSMIC KID: Elvis, is that you?

BOBBY SOXER ELVIS: Yes, it is, Son.

THE COSMIC KID: What happened to you?

BOBBY SOXER ELVIS: Well, Kid, I was like you once. Hair growin' long. Guitar 'round my neck. I even once pissed in my desk at Humes High School in Memphis. But after the Father got done with me with his hypno-therapy, I was able to see the wrong of my ways. Now I'm well on my way to a more righteous path. Soon I'll be in the military. Then I'm going to be making movies. And next, I'll be playing Vegas.

THE COSMIC KID: But you used to be, "Elvis." One of my heroes: you taught me to free my body. I wear this leather jacket because of you.

BOBBY SOXER ELVIS: Oh, trust me, Son. You'll be much happier this way. Watch. For example. When they say, "Sit Down".

FATHER RAY: *(Perhaps in an imitation of Colonel Tom Parker, Elvis's manager)* "Sit down".

BOBBY SOXER ELVIS sits.

BOBBY SOXER ELVIS: I sit down. And when they say "Come down".

FATHER RAY: *(Again, as Colonel Tom)* Come down.

He walks toward them.

ELVIS: I come down. And when they say "Pull down."

FATHER RAY: *(as same)* Pull down.

BOBBY SOXER ELVIS pulls his pants down, and points his ass toward FATHER RAY.

BOBBY SOXER ELVIS: I pull down.

FATHER RAY: Yes, you do… Oh, God, yes you do…

THE COSMIC KID: Oh, Elvis, why?

BOBBY SOXER ELVIS: Life is just easier this way. No more pain. No more rain. I walk the sunny, straight and righteous path.

FATHER RAY: You see, easier. Now look at the silver cross. And life will be easier for you too.

MOTHER: Look, Kid, look…

ELVIS pulls up his pants and starts to exit, as the FATHER begins to move the cross back and forth in front of the KID.

BOBBY SOXER ELVIS: *(Stopping short.)* Oh, Kid, one more thing…

THE COSMIC KID: *(As he begins to fall under the hypno-therapy's spell)* Yeeesssss…

BOBBY SOXER ELVIS: What ever you do: Don't push B-52.

COSMIC KID: *(Snapping alert for a moment)* B-52?

BOBBY SOXER ELVIS: On the Catholic School's Jukebox.

COSMIC KID: The school has a jukebox?

ELVIS: Oh, sure. You know, for those dances where nobody is

allowed to move freely or touch each other.

Lights up on the school's gym, with a special light on a brightly illuminated multi-colored jukebox.

ELVIS: But, I'm warning you: keep your hands off B-52.

THE COSMIC KID: I guess I never noticed the jukebox before. I assumed it was all, "How Much is That Doggie in the Window" and that sort of thing…

FATHER: Well, sure. Nobody ever got too stimulated by "How Much is that Doggie in the Window". Except for Patti Page—who seems awfully into it—and maybe that doggie.

ELVIS: Bye, Kid. B-52.

THE COSMIC KID: B-52…

As THE FATHER moves the cross back and forth, ELVIS gives a small sneer, which is followed by the crash of some cymbals. He then swivels his hips that results in the pounding of some loud drums. The sounds of the percussion give way to lightening and thunder as ELVIS "leaves the building." In that moment, while FATHER RAY continues to move his cross, and the thunder and lightening crash, and the moon above becomes full, and a clock in the gym strikes midnight, a very cartoonish pirate ship comes onto the stage. There is only room aboard the ship for a mast with the Jolly Roger. Clinging to the mast in full pirate regalia, including eye patch and parrot, is THE JUKEBOX GRADUATE, a woman that is the same age as THE COSMIC KID.

FATHER RAY: What the hell?

JUKEBOX GRADUATE: Cosmic Kid? Is that you?

THE COSMIC KID: Cosmic Kid? I'm not the Cosmic Kid. I'm Bruce… Honor student. Captain of the football team. Homecoming King.

JUKEBOX GRADUATE: Cosmic Kid, it's me. The Jukebox Graduate. Your first mate. Remember. Tonight's the night.

You were supposed to meet me out on the turnpike. We were setting sail for points unknown.

KID: I told you… I'm not the Cosmic Kid. I'm Bruce, Esquire. Like my dad wants. I'm Bruce, author, like my mom wants…

JUKEBOX GRADUATE: No, Cosmic Kid, I can't let them do this to you…

THE JUKEBOX GRADUATE grabs holds of a curtain conveniently hanging over the space of Father Ray's office. And in classic Errol Flynn fashion, sweeps the COSMIC KID up off his feet and moves him to the other side of the stage. They are now in front of the jukebox.

FATHER RAY: Well, well, isn't that convenient… But you see, we don't have to rely only on hypno-therapy. We have other means to deal with those of you won't "grow up" in the prescribed manner.

(FATHER RAY takes out a cross-shaped gun.)

The silver bullet in my specially made cross-shaped revolver. It will take what is primal in you and make you something… Else. Now stand back.

MOTHER: Father, no!

FATHER RAY raises the gun to the KID. The end looks near. BOBBY SOXER ELVIS enters.

ELVIS: Don't push B-52….

FATHER: Welcome to the real world… Kid. It's time to grow up…

In a grand gesture, THE KID hits B-52. The jukebox begins to shake and shudder. The lights begin to flash and change. A guitar lowers from the flies in the glow of a spotlight and stops in front of THE COSMIC KID. The song "Heartbreak Hotel" comes roaring out of the jukebox, in a version by Bruce from the '78 tour. THE KID grabs the guitar and with it, and THE JUKEBOX GRADUATE with her sword, they fight FATHER RAY back until he falls to the floor. In that moment: ELVIS is transformed back into the 1950s ELVIS that we revere. THE KID'S MOTHER begins to dance and rock. As, the lights change. The stage goes silent. Slowly a car key is illuminated and begins to lower from the flies. THE KID takes hold of it. The universe seems to illuminate under the fractured light of a mirrored ball. With his hand raised around the key, and an arm around the JUKEBOX GRADUATE, he says:

COSMIC KID: So long, New Jersey. Let it rock!

THEY are raised up off the stage and disappear. As the lights fade to black and the rock and roll gets louder.

End of Play.

COPYRIGHT

Drive All Night

All production inquiries for this play should be directed to Beth Blickers, Agency for the Performing Arts, 135 W. 50th Street, 17th floor, New York, NY 10020; bblickers@apa-agency.com.

Bloody River

All production inquires for this play should be directed to Susan Gurman, Gurman Agency LLC, 14 Penn Plaza, Suite 1703, New York, NY 10026-1701; Susan@gurmanagency.com

a semi-autobiographical response to feelings of sexual inadequacy prompted by repeatedly listening to Bruce Springsteen's "I'm on Fire" over and over for four hours straight

All production inquiries for this play should be directed to Derek Zasky at William Morris Endeavor, at 325 Avenue of the Americas, New York, NY 10019-6026; DZasky@wmeentertainment.com

Glad for the Company

Spirit of Transportation

Merry-Go-Round Man

The Stray

Object Permanence

Gospel Hour

All production inquiries for this play should be sent to Dan Caffrey at dancaffrey@utexas.edu

Valhalla Correctional

All production inquiries for this play should be directed to Susan Gurman, Susan Gurman Agency, LLC 14 Penn Plaza, Suite 1703, New York, NY, 10122; susan@gurmanagency.com

Pick Up Beds

All production inquires for this play should be directed to K. Frithjof Peterson at dandiprat@gmail.com

Birthday Wishes

All production inquiries for this play should visit nikkolesalter.com

Growin' Up, Or I Was A Teenage Springsteen!

All production inquiries for this play should be sent to Dr. Steve Feffer at steve.feffer@wmich.edu

DR. JOAN HERRINGTON is Chair of the Department of Theatre at Western Michigan University and a contemporary theatre scholar whose research is focused on the pedagogy and practice of theatre in the last twenty-five years. She is the author of five books that examine the creative process of playwrights and directors. She has also written more than a dozen books chapters and journal articles appearing in Journal of Dramatic Theory and Criticism, American Drama, and The Drama Review, and she served as editor of the prestigious publication Theatre Topics. Through her research and practice, she has explored modern theatre around the world and engaged theatre artists from Japan to Great Britain to Nigeria. Dr. Herrington has taught workshops at many universities, and her work as a director and dramaturg has taken her from coast to coast with productions in New York and Los Angeles and as far as the Edinburgh Festival in Scotland.